Cambridge English

Garan Holcombe
Series Editor: Annette Capel

Prepare!
WORKBOOK
Level 2

Cambridge University Press
www.cambridge.org/elt

Cambridge English Language Assessment
www.cambridgeenglish.org

Information on this title: www.cambridge.org/9780521180498

© Cambridge University Press and UCLES 2015

This publication is in copyright. Subject to statutory exception
and to the provisions of relevant collective licensing agreements,
no reproduction of any part may take place without the written
permission of the publishers.

First published 2015
6th printing 2016

Printed in Dubai by Oriental Press

A catalogue record for this publication is available from the British Library

ISBN 978-0-521-18048-1 Student's Book
ISBN 978-1-107-49720-7 Student's Book and Online Workbook
ISBN 978-0-521-18049-8 Workbook with Audio
ISBN 978-0-521-18050-4 Teacher's Book with DVD and Teacher's Resources Online
ISBN 978-0-521-18052-8 Class Audio CDs
ISBN 978-1-107-49718-4 Presentation Plus DVD-ROM

The publishers have no responsibility for the persistence or accuracy of URLs
for external or third-party internet websites referred to in this publication, and
do not guarantee that any content on such websites is, or will remain, accurate
or appropriate. Information regarding prices, travel timetables, and other factual
information given in this work is correct at the time of first printing but the
publishers do not guarantee the accuracy of such information thereafter.

Contents

	Get started!	4
1	Sports and games	8
2	Tastes wonderful!	12
3	Great sounds	16
4	A true story	20
5	Fantastic facts	24
6	What a great job!	28
7	Going places	32
8	Special places	36
9	Clothes and fashion	40
10	Buying things	44
11	Eating out	48
12	The latest technology	52
13	Healthy bodies	56
14	In the town	60
15	Weather and places	64
16	Amazing animals	68
17	What's on?	72
18	Papers and magazines	76
19	School can be fun!	80
20	Families	84

Get started!
In the classroom

THINGS IN THE CLASSROOM

1 Complete the words for things in the classroom.

0 p e n c i l   c a s e
1 d _ s k
2 c _ m p _ t _ r
3 b _ _ r d
4 _ x _ r c _ s _
  b _ _ k
5 c h _ _ r
6 b _ g
7 c _ _ t
8 s h _ l f
9 d _ _ r
10 r _ l _ r
11 r _ b b _ r
12 m _ p
13 t _ x t   b _ _ k
14 w _ n d _ w
15 p _ s t _ r

2 Which things in Exercise 1 are in your school bag?

   pencil case
   ....

3 Read the sentences. Write *yes* or *no*.

0 My pencil case is black and white.
   no (My pencil case is blue.)

1 The chairs in my classroom are green.
   ....

2 The classroom door is white.
   ....

3 The board is green.
   ....

4 The desks in my classroom are brown.
   ....

5 My bag is blue and yellow.
   ....

THERE IS / THERE ARE

4 Complete the questions about your classroom with *Is there* or *Are there*.

0 ...Are there... any shelves in your classroom?
1 .... any windows near your desk?
2 .... a computer on the teacher's desk?
3 .... a rubber in your pencil case?
4 .... any maps on the walls in your classroom?
5 .... a door near the board in your classroom?

5 Now write your answers to the questions in Exercise 4.

0 ...Yes, there are. There are two shelves near the window.
1 ....
2 ....
3 ....
4 ....
5 ....

Starter Unit

HAVE GOT

6 Choose the right words to complete the sentences.

0 My mum *have got* / *(has got)* a white bag.
1 I *have got* / *has got* two bottles of water on my desk.
2 My friends *haven't got* / *hasn't got* any money today.
3 This room *haven't got* / *hasn't got* any windows.
4 We *have got* / *has got* some posters on the walls.
5 I *haven't got* / *hasn't got* an exercise book.

7 Put the words in the right order to make questions.

0 you / got / Have / phone / a
   ...Have you got a phone?...
1 got / Have / friends / your / a / football
   ....?
2 your / computer / dad / Has / a / got
   ....?
3 friend / best / Have / got / you / a
   ....?
4 teacher / a / Has / your / got / coat / blue
   ....?
5 you / Have / got / a / pet
   ....?

8 Now write your answers to the questions in Exercise 7.

0 ...Yes, I have.....
1 ....
2 ....
3 ....
4 ....
5 ....

9 What have you got in your school bag? Use these words or your own ideas.

   | textbook   exercise book   a bottle of water
   | football   pencil case   money   phone

In my school bag I've got ....
....
....
....

THE ALPHABET

10 Say these letters. Then circle the letter with the different sound.

0 A H Ⓖ
1 F G X
2 Q U V
3 D P S
4 J K R
5 E I Y

SPEAKING

11 Choose the right words to complete the conversations.

1 **A:** How do you *say* / *spell* 'different'?
  B: D-I-F-F-E-R-E-N-T.
2 **A:** What *page* / *book* are we on?
  B: 19, I think.
3 **A:** How do you *say* / *spell* 'gracias' in English?
  B: Thank you.
4 **A:** Can I *take* / *borrow* your rubber?
  B: Sure, here you are.
5 **A:** I'm sorry, can you *repeat* / *spell* that please?
  B: I said, please do Exercise 3.

Get started!

Talk about you

NUMBERS

1 Write the numbers.

7	............seven............
.........9.........	nine
14	....
....	eighteen
20	....
....	twenty-three
31	....
....	forty
56	....
....	sixty-two
71	....
....	eighty-five
90	....
....	a hundred

DATES

2 Put the letters in the right order to make months.

0 A i l p r	............April............
1 b e e e m p r S t	....
2 l J u y	....
3 a c h M r	....
4 A g s t u u	....
5 a M y	....
6 b c D e e e m r	....
7 e J n u	....
8 a a J n r u y	....
9 b c e O o r t	....
10 a b e F r r u y	....
11 b e e m N o r v	....

3 Now write the months in Exercise 2 in the right order.

1 ....January............
2 ....
3 ....
4 ....
5 ....
6 ....
7 ....
8 ....
9 ....
10 ....
11 ....
12 ....December............

4 Answer the questions and write the dates.

0 When's your teacher's birthday?
   ....Her birthday is on 21st March.....

1 When's your birthday?
   ....

2 When's your best friend's birthday?
   ....

3 What's today's date?
   ....

4 What's tomorrow's date?
   ....

5 When's the next holiday?
   ....

CAN

5 Match the words.

0 draw	a a bike
1 make	b a cake
2 play	c a picture
3 ride	d three languages
4 run	e tennis
5 speak	f on your head
6 stand	g under water
7 swim	h 5k

(0 draw — c a picture)

6 Use the words in Exercise 5 to write questions.

0 ....Can you draw a picture?....
1 ....
2 ....
3 ....
4 ....
5 ....

6 Starter Unit

7 Now write your answers to the questions in Exercise 6.

0 Yes, I can.
1 ....
2 ....
3 ....
4 ....
5 ....

8 Now complete these sentences with the words in Exercise 5 or use your own ideas.

0 I can ride a bike but I can't stand on my head.
1 I can .... but I can't ....
2 My mum can .... but she can't ....
3 My friends can .... but they can't ....

PRESENT SIMPLE

9 Complete this text with the present simple form of the verbs.

Hi, my name (0) is Jack.
I (1) .... (have got) a brother and a sister. I (2) .... (like) music and I (3) .... (love) travelling. Ravi and Molly are my friends. Ravi (4) .... (not have got) any brothers or sisters and Molly (5) .... (have got) one sister. Ravi (6) .... (like) all sports and he (7) .... (play) football every day. Molly (8) .... (not play) football. She (9) .... (like) swimming.

10 Put the words in the right order to make questions.

1 books / What / of / like / kind / you / do
....?
2 you / Do / pictures / like / drawing
....?
3 school / What / do / sports / play / you / at
....?
4 watching / like / you / Do / TV
....?
5 animal / What / favourite / your / is
....?

11 Now write your answers to the questions in Exercise 10.

1 ....
2 ....
3 ....
4 ....
5 ....

12 Complete these sentences for you.

Hello, my name's ....
I've got ....
I like .... and I love ....

SPEAKING

13 Match the questions to the answers.

0 How old are you? ...d...
1 What's your address? ....
2 What's your phone number? ....
3 Have you got any brothers or sisters? ....
4 Who's your favourite pop star? ....
5 What's your favourite school subject? ....

a Yes, I've got two sisters.
b It's 13 Green Road.
c It's Rihanna
d I'm 13.
e I love maths.
f It's 477888

14 Now use the questions in Exercise 13 to write about your best friend.

My best friend is ....
....
....
....
....
....

1 Sports and games
I'm never bored

VOCABULARY

1 Look at the pictures and write the words.

> badminton   baseball   cycling   hockey   ~~rugby~~
> running   sailing   skating   snowboarding   volleyball

0 rugby   1 ....   2 ....   3 ....

4 ....   5 ....   6 ....   7 ....

8 ....   9 ....

2 Now complete the table with the words from Exercise 1.

play	go
rugby	....
....	....
....	....
....	....
....	....

3 Choose the right word to complete the sentences.

0 My sister (plays) / goes volleyball at the weekend.
1 My friends John and Toby play / go sailing in the summer.
2 We play / go running in the evening.
3 My brother plays / goes hockey on Sundays.
4 I don't play / go badminton with my friends.
5 Do you play / go snowboarding alone?

Unit 1

GRAMMAR Adverbs of frequency

4 Put the words in the right order to make questions.

0 do / go / in / often / you / the / running / summer
Do you often go running in the summer?

1 get / do / always / early / you / up
....?

2 in / films / English / watch / you / do / sometimes
....?

3 you / always / in / homework / the / your / do / do / evening
....?

4 for / you / sometimes / family / dinner / do / your / cook
....?

5 summer / your / always / holiday / go / on / family / the / in / does
....?

5 Now write your answers to the questions in Exercise 4.

0 No, I don't. I never go running in the summer.

1 ....
2 ....
3 ....
4 ....
5 ....

6 Write the adverb in the right space.

0 I ..never.. watch football ..—.. on TV. I don't like it. (never)

1 My sister .... goes .... to the cinema at the weekend. (usually)

2 I'm .... late for .... school. (sometimes)

3 My friends .... go .... snowboarding in the winter. (often)

4 I .... see my grandparents .... on Sundays. (always)

7 👁 Students often make mistakes with the position of adverbs of frequency. Correct the mistakes in these sentences.

0 In the morning usually we have bread with butter and jam.
In the morning we usually have bread with butter and jam.

1 I drink juice always.
....

2 For dinner often we have pasta.
....

3 In my free time usually I stay at home.
....

4 I go often to the cinema with my friends.
....

5 I go always there when it's summer.
....

LISTENING

8 ▶2 Listen to the interview with the teen sports star Andrea Murray. Match the people to the sports.

0 Andrea — a volleyball
1 Sandra — b tennis
2 Tony   c rugby
3 Dan   d badminton and sailing
4 Amy   e snowboarding and skating

9 ▶2 Listen to the interview again. Are the sentences right (✓) or wrong (✗)?

0 Andrea listens to Barry's podcast. ✓
1 She often gets up late. ....
2 She plays tennis for three hours before school. ....
3 She gets up at five o'clock on Wednesdays. ....
4 She plays tennis all day on Sundays. ....
5 She goes to the cinema with her friends in her free time. ....

10 Write five questions to ask Andrea.

0 Who is your favourite tennis player?
1 ....
2 ....
3 ....
4 ....
5 ....

Sports and games

How do you play it?

VOCABULARY

1 Find six sports words.

f	s	a	i	l	i	n	g
k	o	m	w	p	r	x	e
g	a	o	r	t	s	c	t
s	w	c	t	a	r	l	e
b	t	o	f	b	a	t	a
g	j	i	t	i	a	s	m
d	h	w	c	p	f	l	l
l	r	a	c	k	e	t	l

2 Now complete the sentences with the words from Exercise 1.

0 Hockey players hit the ball with a s. *tick* .
1 You use a small r....................... when you play tennis.
2 The Los Angeles Lakers are a famous basketball t....................... .
3 Baseball players use a b....................... to hit the ball.
4 You need a boat to go s....................... .
5 Manchester United are an English f....................... team.

3 Read the sentences about rugby. Choose the best word (A, B or C) for each space.

Example:
0 People ..*C*.... rugby all over the world.
   A do   B go   C play
1 There are 15 people in a rugby ....
   A goal   B band   C team
2 Rugby players use a ....
   A ball   B match   C group
3 They never .... a stick, bat or racket.
   A use   B hit   C play
4 Players run with the ball in their ....
   A legs   B feet   C hands
5 Players .... the ball too.
   A hit   B kick   C run

10 Unit 1

WRITING

4 Match the descriptions to the sports.

a golf
b cricket
c basketball
d volleyball

1 You play this sport inside or outside. There are six people in a team. Players hit the ball with their hands across a net.

2 People play this sport alone or in teams. They play it with clubs – they're like hockey sticks. Players hit a small ball into nine or eighteen holes.

3 Players in this sport are usually tall. There are five people in a team. Players have to throw the ball through a net to score points.

4 People play this sport by hitting a red ball with a bat. There are eleven players in a team and players wear white clothes. They sometimes wear unusual hats. People usually play this sport in the spring and summer.

5 Find these adjectives in the descriptions. Write the nouns.

0 small ....ball.......
1 tall ....
2 red ....
3 white ....
4 unusual ....

6 Now write about your favourite sport. Use adjectives.

....
....
....
....
....
....
....

Sports and games 11

2 Tastes wonderful!
Today I'm making pancakes

VOCABULARY

1 Find the odd one out.

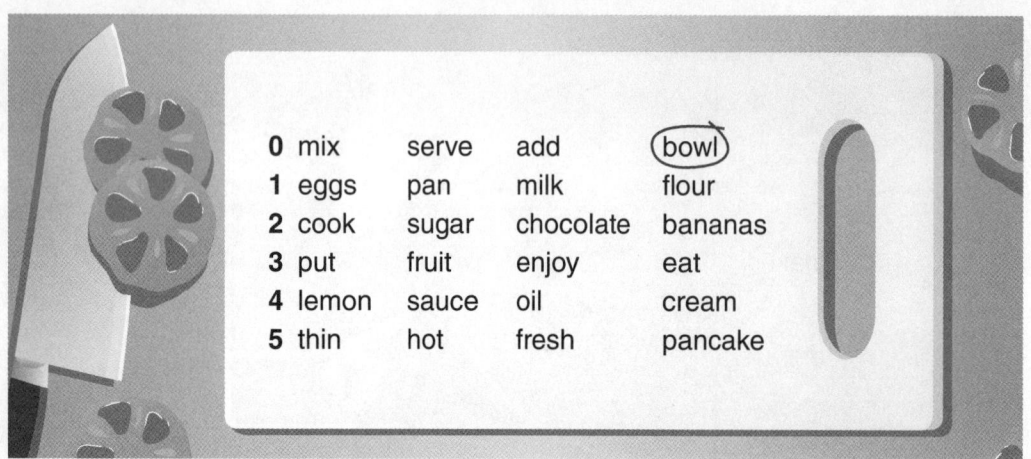

```
0  mix     serve    add        (bowl)
1  eggs    pan      milk       flour
2  cook    sugar    chocolate  bananas
3  put     fruit    enjoy      eat
4  lemon   sauce    oil        cream
5  thin    hot      fresh      pancake
```

2 Complete the table with the food words.

mix, oil, serve, bowl, pan, enjoy, sauce, lemon, add, thin, fresh, cook, cream, put, hot, pancake

Nouns	Verbs	Adjectives
......	......	......
......	......	......
......	......	......
......	......	......
......	......	......
......	......	......

3 Now complete the text with words from Exercise 2.

I (0) ..enjoy.. cooking. I (1) .... every day for my family. I like making sweet things. My favourite thing to make is chocolate cake. I put flour, oil, sugar and eggs in a (2) .... and (3) .... them together. Then I (4) .... lots of chocolate. I put it in the oven for an hour and serve it with (5) ....

GRAMMAR Present continuous and present simple

4 Match the two halves of the sentences.

0 She's making a pizza —   a cooking now?
1 What do you usually   b chocolate sauce today.
2 As you can see, I'm serving the cakes with   c do in the evenings?
3 What is your brother   d on Sundays.
4 I always serve pancakes   e at the moment.
5 We never go to restaurants   f with fresh fruit.

5 Circle the right word or phrase to complete the sentences.

1 We *always / at the moment* eat pancakes on Saturdays, but never on Sundays.
2 My brother is making a pizza *now / usually*. It's his favourite food!
3 Why have you got your maths book, Daisy? We're studying English *often / today*.
4 What are you doing *sometimes / at the moment*? Are you doing your homework?
5 I *usually / at the moment* go to bed at nine o'clock from Monday to Friday. At the weekend I go to bed at ten!
6 My grandmother *now / always* makes beautiful cakes.

6 Complete the sentences with the words in the box.

| doing | playing | watching |
| does | ~~plays~~ | watch |

0 He ...plays... the piano every day.
1 What are you .... at the moment?
2 They .... films at the weekend.
3 My brother's .... the guitar now.
4 They're .... a film at the moment.
5 She .... her homework every evening.

7 👁 Students often make mistakes with the present continuous. Correct the mistakes in these sentences.

1 It rains a lot at the moment.
....
2 I travel by bus and I will arrive on Saturday at 9 am.
....
3 You know that I paint my bedroom.
....
4 I'm sorry I can't go to the birthday party because I go to the hospital.
....
5 I like singing. I'm singing in the school hall.
....

LISTENING

8 ▶3 Listen to the conversation between Jane and George. Who says what? Write *J* for Jane and *G* for George.

0 I never see you in the supermarket on Tuesdays. ....G....
1 What are you buying today? ....
2 I don't usually buy crisps, sweets or chocolate. ....
3 My sister is home from university. ....
4 My little brother loves pancakes. ....
5 I love pancakes too! ....

9 ▶3 Listen again and answer the questions.

0 When does Jane usually go shopping with her parents?
...Wednesdays and Saturdays...
1 When does George usually go shopping with his parents?
....
2 Who likes sweets, crisps and chocolate?
....
3 When does George eat chocolate?
....
4 What is George buying today?
....
5 What does George serve pancakes with?
....

Tastes wonderful!

Lunch is always at midday

VOCABULARY

1 Look at the pictures and write the words.

> cabbage   cereal   chilli   cucumber   curry and rice   fruit tea
> honey   hot chocolate   jam   mango   salad   toast   yogurt

1 chilli

2 jam

3 mango

4 fruit tea

5 cabbage

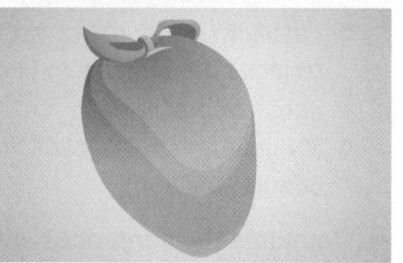

6 yogurt

7 hot chocolate

8 honey

9 salad

10 toast

11 cereal

12 cucumber

13 curry and rice

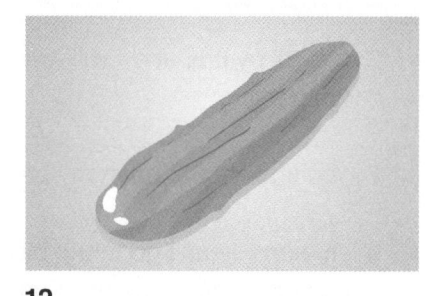

2 Now match the food words to the sentences.

1 fruit tea   a We eat this for breakfast.
2 toast   b This is a drink.
3 chilli   c This is a green vegetable.
4 cabbage   d This is a sweet fruit.
5 mango   e This is red or green and is sometimes very hot.

3 Put the words in the right order to make sentences.

1 for / breakfast / cereal / she / has
....

2 likes / on / toast / jam / he
....

3 morning / every / I / fruit tea / drink
....

4 the / eat / summer / in / we / salad
....

5 the / in / evenings / hot chocolate / drink / they
....
....

4 Read the descriptions of some words about food. What is the word for each one? The first letter is already there. There is one space for each other letter in the word.

Example:
0 This is sweet and yellow, and you eat it on toast.   h o n e y
1 People usually eat this with milk for breakfast.   c _ _ _ _ _
2 This is made from fruit and sugar.   j _ _
3 We don't usually cook this long, thin, green vegetable.   c _ _ _ _ _ _ _
4 It is good to eat this cold food in hot weather.   s _ _ _ _
5 You can add more chilli to make this food very hot.   c _ _ _ _

Prepare to write

5 Choose the right word to complete the sentences.

1 I don't like pancakes *or* / *but* chocolate.
2 I eat lots of fish *or* / *and* drink lots of tea.
3 My sister likes bananas *and* / *but* she doesn't like apples.
4 My brother likes curry *but* / *and* rice.
5 I don't eat honey *and* / *but* I like jam.
6 My dad likes fruit *and* / *or* vegetables.

6 Complete the text with *and*, *but* and *or*.

My family loves food! We eat a lot of great meals. My mum (1) .... dad can cook, (2) .... my grandmother is the best cook in the family. We eat meat for dinner on Mondays, Tuesdays, Wednesdays (3) .... Thursdays, and fish on Fridays. At the weekend we go to restaurants. I like Italian food, (4) .... my parents don't. They don't like pizza (5) .... pasta! They prefer Mexican food.

7 Now write about what your family eats. Use *and*, *but* and *or*.

....
....
....
....
....
....
....

Tastes wonderful! 15

3 Great sounds
I love listening to rap

VOCABULARY

1 Put the letters in the right order to make music words.

0 o p p ....pop........

1 p a r ....

2 o p n i a ....

3 c o r k ....

4 s m u d r ....

5 z a z j ....

6 c l l a a c i s s ....

7 r a t i g u ....

8 l u s o ....

9 n i o l i v ....

10 b e y d a r o k ....

2 ▶4 Listen to and complete the text with the words in the box.

| fun | ~~instruments~~ | loud | plays | types |

Hello and welcome to the City School of Music. My name's Robert and I'm a student here. Everyone at the school plays lots of musical (0) ...instruments... . And we all learn to play different (1) .... of music. Tommy (2) .... the guitar in a band. The band is really (3) ....! I'm in the band too! I play the drums. It's lots of (4) ....

GRAMMAR like, don't like, hate, love + -ing

3 Number the sentences in the right order 1 (☺) to 6 (☹).

a I quite like learning English. ....
b I hate learning English. ....
c I like learning English. ....
d I really love learning English. ....1....
e I don't like learning English. ....
f I love learning English. ....

4 Write complete sentences.

0 My mother / love / cook
   My mother loves cooking.
1 My brother / not like / do / homework
   ....
2 I / hate / play / video games
   ....
3 My sister / really love / watch / films
   ....
4 My best friend / like / read / books
   ....
5 My father / quite like / play / table tennis
   ....

5 Correct the spelling mistakes in these sentences.

0 I really love writting stories.
   I really love writing stories.
1 My friends don't like runing.
   ....
2 I hate geting the bus to school.
   ....
3 My family enjoys makeing pizza.
   ....
4 My brother quite likes listenning to music.
   ....
5 I like swiming in the sea.
   ....

6 👁 Students often make mistakes with *like, don't like, hate, love* + *-ing*. Correct the mistakes in these sentences. Two of the sentences are correct.

1 I like doing shopping with her.
   ....
2 He doesn't like watching football on TV.
   ....
3 I don't like play football at school.
   ....
4 She like talking.
   ....
5 We love listening to music.
   ....

WRITING

7 Read the text and answer the questions.

My name's Kate and I'm thirteen years old. My friends and I all love music. I like classical but I don't like pop. Sienna really loves pop and rock. Ewan doesn't like rock but he quite likes rap. He loves classical. Jonny hates jazz but he likes rock. He doesn't like rap but he likes classical. My friends and I love listening to music but our favourite thing is playing music. We have a band called The Pink Elephants!

0 Who likes rock?
   Jonny
1 Who doesn't like pop?
   ....
2 Who really loves pop?
   ....
3 Who quite likes rap?
   ....
4 Who loves classical?
   ....
5 Who hates jazz?
   ....

8 Now write about the music that you and your friends like or don't like.

....
....
....
....
....
....
....
....

Great sounds 17

This is the MAD school

VOCABULARY Words that go together

1 Choose the right word or phrase.
1 become *famous* / *on stage*
2 give *a concert* / *in a band*
3 play *famous* / *in a band*
4 become *an actor* / *a concert*
5 dance *on stage* / *an album*
6 teach *a concert* / *music*
7 record *famous* / *an album*

2 Complete the sentences with the verbs from Exercise 1 in the correct form.
1 My history teacher .... in a rock band.
2 My sister wants to .... famous.
3 My mother .... music in a school in Barcelona. Her students love her!
4 Tamara likes .... on stage. She does salsa and tango.
5 Does your cousin want to .... an album with her band?
6 My friends have a band and like .... concerts for their families.
7 My brother wants to .... an actor.

LISTENING

3 ▶5 **You will hear Sam asking about violin lessons. Listen and complete Sam's notes.**

VIOLIN LESSONS

Teacher's name:	Mrs Driscoll
Time of lessons:	(1) ....
Days of lessons:	(2) .... and Fridays
Price of lessons:	(3) £ .... an hour
Teacher's house:	(4) near the ....
Teacher's phone number:	(5) ....

Unit 3

READING

4 Complete the text with the words in the box.

famous   students   become   subjects

Stage schools

At a stage school, young people learn how to (1) .... actors, dancers and singers. There are many stage schools in the UK. One of the most (2) .... stage schools is the Sylvia Young Theatre School in London. There are 250 students at the school. Children aged between ten and sixteen go there.

At Sylvia Young Theatre School (3) .... learn all of the subjects, like maths, history and science, which students learn at secondary schools. They do these (4) .... on Mondays, Tuesdays and Wednesdays. Then they dance, sing and act on Thursdays and Fridays. There aren't any lessons on Saturdays or Sundays.

5 Read the text again. Are the sentences right (✓) or wrong (✗)?

1 There aren't many stage schools in the UK. ....
2 There are 350 students at the Sylvia Young Theatre School. ....
3 Twelve-year-old children can study at the Sylvia Young Theatre School. ....
4 Students study maths at the Sylvia Young Theatre School. ....
5 Students learn how to sing, dance and act on Saturdays. ....

6 Now read the text again and answer the questions.

1 What do young people learn to do at stage schools?
....
2 Where is the Sylvia Young Theatre School?
....
3 How many students are there at the Sylvia Young Theatre School?
....
4 Do students learn subjects like geography and languages at the stage school?
....
5 What do students do on Thursdays and Fridays?
....

Great sounds 19

4 A true story
The missing ring

VOCABULARY Describing things

1 Complete the words for shapes and materials.

0 w o o d
1 s _ l v _ r
2 g _ l d
3 p l _ s t _ c
4 s q _ _ r _
5 r _ _ _ d

2 Are the sentences right (✔) or wrong (✘)?

1 The earth is square. ....
2 Necklaces are often made of silver. ....
3 Bags are sometimes made of plastic. ....
4 Boxes are round. ....
5 Tables and chairs are never made of wood. ....
6 Rings are sometimes made of gold. ....

3 Put the words in the right order to make questions.

1 of / made / ring / your / is / what
....?
2 of / silver / made / earrings / are / your
....?
3 of / necklace / gold / made / is / your
....?
4 describe / it / can / you
....?

4 👁 Students often make mistakes with *it's made of …* . Correct the mistakes in these sentences. Two of the sentences are correct.

1 In the summer I prefer wide trousers of natural material.
....
....

2 My grandmother's ring is made of silver.
....

3 This old table is made of wood.
....

4 I really like clothes of cotton.
....

5 Cuzco is a historical place. You can find lots of things of gold and silver.
....
....

LISTENING

5 ▶6 Listen and match the prices to the objects.
1 £4.99   a earrings
2 £24.99   b necklace
3 £49.99   c rings

6 ▶6 Listen again and choose the right answer.
0 What is the name of the TV presenter?
   a Albert White   (b) Alfie Wise
1 What is the name of the TV show?
   a The Shopping Show   b Shop Till You Drop
2 What is the name of the guest?
   a Martha Blue   b Marta Shoe
3 What is the necklace made of?
   a gold   b silver
4 What are the earrings made of?
   a plastic   b silver
5 What are the rings like?
   a small and white   b big and bright

VOCABULARY

7 Read the sentences about rings.
Choose the best word (A, B or C) for each space.

Example:
0 Most people .... to wear rings.
   (A) love   B enjoy   C show
1 Rings are .... made of gold, but there are plastic ones too.
   A often   B always   C never
2 Gold rings are usually very ....
   A busy   B expensive   C free
3 Plastic rings are .... than silver ones.
   A shorter   B older   C cheaper
4 Grandparents .... rings to younger people in their family.
   A go   B get   C give
5 Students can sometimes .... rings with the name of their university.
   A buy   B serve   C cost

A true story

How surprised were you?

GRAMMAR was / were ➕ ➖ ❓

1 Circle the right word to complete the sentences.

1 I *was / were* at the beach with my family yesterday.
2 We *was / were* in the cinema at six o'clock.
3 *Was / Were* you at Sam's party on Saturday?
4 It *wasn't / weren't* hot in Scotland last week.
5 He *was / were* my teacher last year.

2 Rewrite the sentences in the past.

0 It isn't sunny.
   ...It wasn't sunny...

1 The ring is in the lake.
   ....

2 I'm very happy.
   ....

3 We aren't at school.
   ....

4 She isn't at the park.
   ....

VOCABULARY how + adjective

3 Match the questions to the answers below.

1 How tall is the Eiffel Tower?
2 How cold is it in Siberia in the winter?
3 How long is a pencil?
4 How hot is it in Cairo in the summer?
5 How far is it from London to Paris?

a 35 degrees   ....
b 324 metres   ....
c –20 degrees   ....
d 213 kilometres ....
e 19 centimetres ....

4 Choose the right word to complete the questions.

1 How *clever / old* is the tree?
2 How *long / tall* is your sister?
3 How *funny / tired* was the film?
4 How *hot / big* was it at the beach?
5 How *dirty / difficult* was the French test?

5 Match the two halves to make questions.

1 How difficult   a is your town?
2 How clever   b are you?
3 How tall   c was the exam?
4 How funny   d is your brother?
5 How big   e was the party?
6 How exciting   f was the film?

Prepare to write

6 Choose the right words to complete the sentences.

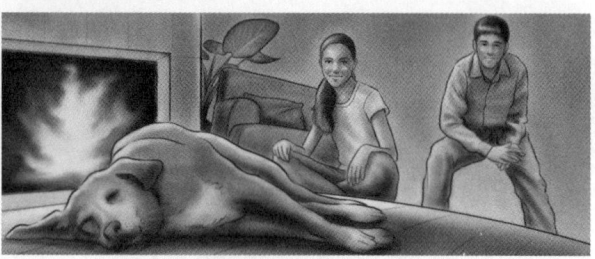

1 We've got a *nice new / tired old* dog.

2 My sister wears a *big old / small white* hat.

3 My cousin drives a *tired old / big black* racing car.

4 We live in a *big black / nice new* house.

5 My sister uses a *small white / big old* phone.

7 Match the descriptions to three of the objects in the pictures.

1 This is small. It's made of wood. We sit on it. ....
2 This is white. It's made of paper. We read it. ....
3 This is round and beautiful. It's made of gold. We wear it. ....

8 Write about the other two objects in Exercise 5. Use adjectives.

5 Fantastic facts
Neil Armstrong walked on the moon

VOCABULARY

1 Find ten verbs.

w	r	e	c	o	r	d	c
p	a	t	e	x	t	o	l
p	l	l	j	d	b	p	i
a	g	a	k	o	j	e	m
i	a	l	y	h	i	n	b
n	p	m	y	e	l	n	r
t	c	r	o	s	s	j	z
c	o	m	p	l	e	t	e

2 Complete the text with the verbs in the box.

climbed   completed   painted   played   texted

My brother is always busy at the weekends! For example, last Saturday he was very busy. In the morning he (1) .... his bedroom walls and in the afternoon he (2) .... a new computer program. He's very good with computers. On Sunday morning he (3) .... three of his friends on his new phone and then he (4) .... tennis with them. On Sunday afternoon he (5) .... a mountain near our home. I don't know how he does it all!

3 Complete the sentences with *in* or *on*.

1 Lionel Messi played his first match for Barcelona .... 16th October 2004.
2 Lady Gaga recorded her first album .... 2008.
3 Apple opened its first store .... 19th May 2001.
4 Da Vinci painted the Mona Lisa .... the 16th century.
5 Gareth Bale joined Real Madrid .... 2013.

GRAMMAR   Past simple: regular verbs

4 Write the past simple form of the verbs.

1 travel   ....
2 want   ....
3 stay   ....
4 decide   ....
5 complete ....
6 climb   ....
7 cross   ....
8 visit   ....
9 play   ....
10 join   ....

5 Write past simple sentences.

Every week ...

0 I help my parents at home.
1 I practise the guitar.
2 I clean the bathroom.
3 I play basketball with my friends.
4 I phone my grandmother.
5 I study maths, English and history.

Last week ...

0 I helped my parents at home.
1 ....
2 ....
3 ....
4 ....
5 ....

Diary

6 Match the two halves of the sentences.

1 I watched a
2 My mother
3 I studied
4 My brother cooked
5 I practised

a played table tennis yesterday. She's very good at it.
b the piano every day last week. I like playing.
c spaghetti for us on Friday. It was very nice.
d for my geography exam at the weekend.
e film with friends last night. It was very funny.

7 Students often make mistakes with verbs in the past simple. Correct the mistakes in these sentences.

1 I had quite a nice time. I play some games.
....
2 I went with my cousins to the mountains and we climb the hill.
....
3 Some days it was too hot but on others it rain.
....
4 The weather was very bad, it was very cold, it snow.
....
5 Yesterday I watch a football competition with Carol.
....

The Great Fire of London

VOCABULARY

1 Read the descriptions of some words about the Great Fire of London. What is the word for each one? The first letter is already there. There is one space for each other letter in the word.

Example:

0 This animal looks like a mouse and has a long tail. r <u>a</u> <u>t</u>

1 A house, a church and a school are all examples of this. b _ _ _ _ _ _ _

2 When there are too many people in a room you say that it is this. c _ _ _ _ _ _ _

3 Trees are made of this. w _ _ _

4 This means the same as ill. s _ _ _

5 This is another word for a road in a town or city. s _ _ _ _ _

2 Now complete the sentences with the words from Exercise 1.

1 My grandmother has a beautiful old table made of ....

2 My mother works in a new .... near the river.

3 My house is in the same .... as my school.

4 I couldn't go to school last week because I was ....

5 I don't like .... buses.

6 There was a .... in our kitchen last night! It was horrible!

LISTENING

3 ▶7 Listen to 'Freddie's Fabulous Facts'. Match the children to the famous people they hear about.

1 Robert   a Pelé
2 Lisa   b Henry VIII
3 Rachel   c Buzz Aldrin
4 Leon   d Sir Francis Drake

4 ▶7 Listen again. Tick (✓) the facts you hear and cross (✗) the ones you don't hear.

0 King Henry VIII of England died in 1587. ......✗....

1 Henry VIII had six wives. ....

2 The footballer Pelé played for Santos 605 times. ....

3 Pelé played for Brazil 92 times. ....

4 The explorer Sir Francis Drake travelled around the world in the 16th century. ....

5 Sir Francis Drake died in Panama. ....

6 The astronaut Buzz Aldrin landed on the moon in 1969. ....

7 Buzz Aldrin was the second man to walk on the moon. ....

26   Unit 5

WRITING

5 Complete the blog with the verbs in the box.

| climbed | played | stayed | visited |

DAISY'S Weekend Blog

My family went to London at the weekend. What a city!

We (1) .... in a beautiful hotel near Covent Garden in the centre of the city for three nights. On Saturday morning we (2) .... to the top of St Paul's Cathedral. We took lots of photos!

On Sunday morning we (3) .... the Tower of London and the Tate Modern museum. The Tate is an interesting building near the River Thames.

On Sunday afternoon we (4) .... football in Hyde Park. It was a very sunny day! We went home on Monday morning, but we all wanted to stay in London!

6 Match the names of famous things in London to the words.

1 Hyde   **a** cathedral
2 Tate Modern   **b** park
3 St Paul's   **c** river
4 Thames   **d** museum

7 Now write about your weekend. Use the past simple of some of these verbs.

climb	complete	cook	copy	cross
dance	enjoy	finish	help	join
invite	open	paint	phone	play
record	study	travel	visit

Fantastic facts

6 What a great job!
Where did you work?

VOCABULARY

1 Complete the table with the words in the box.

> boss   busy   close   computer   customer   desk   earn   finish
> friendly   happy   office   open   nice   staff   start   work   worried

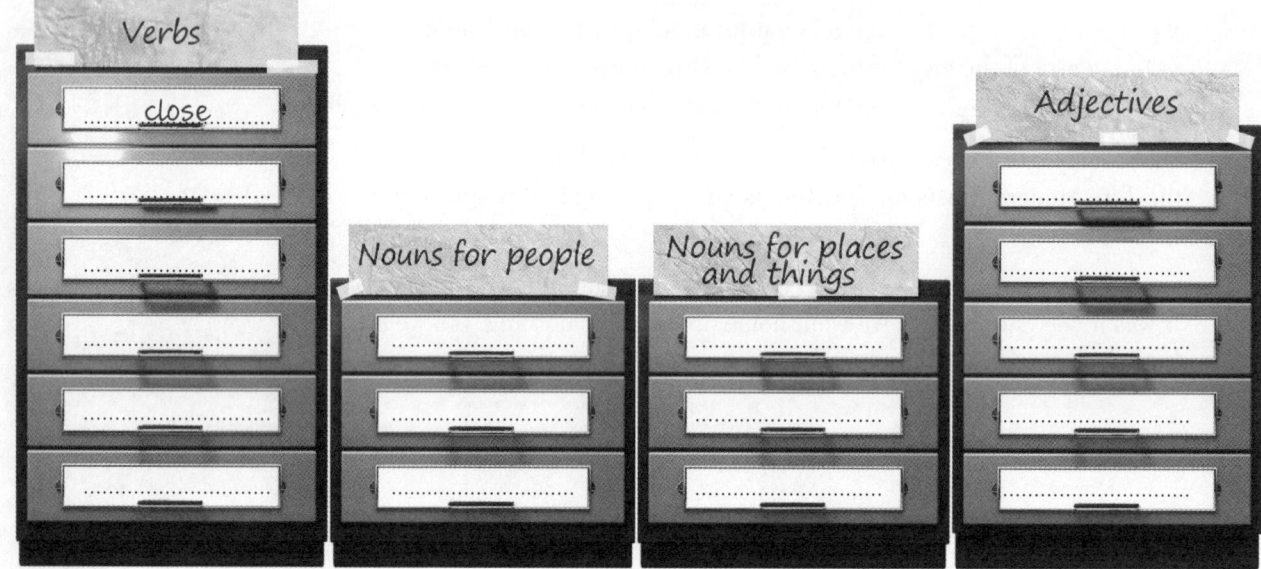

2 Choose the right word to complete the sentences.

1 My *boss / staff* is really nice.
2 I would like to *start / earn* a lot of money.
3 My father works in a very big *computer / office* in the centre of town.
4 I was very *worried / happy* at work because the people were nice.
5 We were very *busy / friendly* at work yesterday. We didn't have time for lunch.
6 The shop *closed / finished* at seven o'clock.

GRAMMAR   Past simple: questions and negatives

3 Put the words in the right order to make questions.

1 time / did / open / the / what / shop
   .... ?
2 did / think / what / customer / the
   .... ?
3 work / yesterday / to / go / did / you
   .... ?
4 the / week / come / did / office / she / to / last
   .... ?
5 did / yesterday / what / do / staff / the
   .... ?
6 he / did / job / his / enjoy
   .... ?

4 Now match the questions in Exercise 3 to the answers.

a Yes, I did.   ....3....
b No, he didn't.   ....
c They phoned all our customers.   ....
d Yes, she did.   ....
e He wasn't very happy about it.   ....
f At six o'clock.   ....

5 Complete the sentences with the negative form of the verbs in the box.

| cleaned | earned | finished |
| learned | phoned | watched |

1 I .... my homework yesterday evening.
2 My grandfather .... French at school.
3 My sister .... much money.
4 We .... the kitchen or the bathroom.
5 I .... my grandmother yesterday.
6 My parents .... the film.

6 👁 **Students often make mistakes with verbs in the past simple. Correct the mistakes in these sentences. Two of the sentences are correct.**

1 The weather was very cold. I don't like the weather.
   ....
2 I went to Tokyo in Japan. The weather was windy.
   ....
3 I help my dad last week.
   ....
4 Do you see the sports championship yesterday?
   ....
5 Did you buy a mobile at the weekend?
   ....

LISTENING

7 ▶8 You will hear five short conversations. There is one question for each conversation. For each question, choose the right answer (A, B or C).

Example:
0 Where did Ronnie work?

 A ☐  B ✓  C ☐

1 How did Hazel get to the shop?

 A ☐  B ☐  C ☐

2 Why did Ali like the job?

 A ☐  B ☐  C ☐

3 What time did Jane start work?

 A ☐  B ☐  C ☐

4 What did Michael wear?

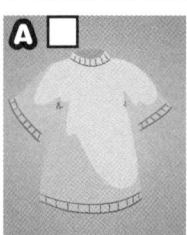 A ☐ 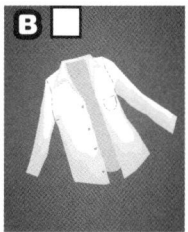 B ☐  C ☐

5 Who was in the group with Ken?

 A ☐  B ☐  C ☐

What a great job!

50 different jobs!

VOCABULARY

1 What jobs do the people do? Complete the sentences with *a* or *an* and the words in the box.

> car mechanic   cook   engineer   farmer
> ~~factory worker~~   fisherman   football coach
> model   photographer   TV weather man

0 I work in a factory.
I'm *a factory worker*.

1 I look after animals.
I'm ....

2 I build things.
I'm ....

3 I work with cars.
I'm ....

4 I tell people about the weather.
I'm ....

5 I work with a football team.
I'm ....

6 People take photographs of me.
I'm ....

7 I work on a boat at sea.
I'm ....

8 I make food.
I'm ....

9 I take photographs.
I'm ....

READING

2 Complete the text with jobs from Exercise 1.

> We talked about jobs at school today. John knows everything about sport. He wants to be a (1) .... Edgar wants to be a farmer. He loves animals! Lee wants to be a (2) .... because he likes helping his parents in the kitchen. Warren wants to be photographer. He always has his camera with him. Marina wants to be an (3) .... because she's very good at drawing and making things. Julie wants to be a mechanic. Cars are her favourite thing. What about me? I don't know what I want to do. Sometimes, I think I want to be a (4) .... because I like the sea.

3 Read the text again. Are the sentences right (✔) or wrong (✘)?

0 John hates football. ......✘......
1 Edgar doesn't like animals. ....
2 Lee doesn't like cooking. ....
3 Warren has got a camera. ....
4 Marina enjoys drawing. ....
5 Julie is interested in cars. ....

Prepare to write

4 Write the text with capital letters, apostrophes and full stops.

> **my grandmothers job**
>
> my grandmother worked in an office she started work at nine o'clock and she finished at five o'clock she didnt earn a lot of money, but she enjoyed her job the people were very friendly and good fun my grandmother used a computer at work for the first time in 1981 thats a long time ago! there were phones in the office, but there werent any mobiles everything is different now my grandmother uses a tablet computer and a smart phone every day!

5 Read the text again and match the two halves of the sentences.

1 My grandmother worked   **a** any mobiles in her office.
2 She finished work   **b** in an office.
3 She enjoyed   **c** at five o'clock.
4 There weren't   **d** earn much money.
5 She didn't   **e** her job.

6 Now write about a job that one of your grandparents did.

7 Going places
We went to Turkey on holiday

VOCABULARY

1 Match the verbs to the nouns to make holiday phrases.

1	go	a	presents
2	stay at a	b	sightseeing
3	buy	c	bike
4	take	d	camping
5	swim in the	e	hotel
6	go	f	beach
7	ride a	g	photos
8	go to the	h	sea

2 Complete the sentences. Use the holiday phrases from Exercise 1 and put the verbs in the correct form.

1 I don't like .... because it's always very cold at night.
2 We sometimes .... before breakfast. The water is usually cold!
3 I love .... because I'm interested in famous old buildings and monuments.
4 My father never .... any .... He doesn't like cameras.
5 We .... great .... on our holiday. Our room was really big!
6 We always .... in the summer. There is one near our house.
7 I sometimes .... when we go on holiday. I like going fast!
8 Did you .... any .... from the shop? I bought a book for my friend.

GRAMMAR   Past simple: irregular verbs

3 Find the verbs.

Unit 7

4 Complete the sentences with verbs from Exercise 3.

1 I .... on holiday to Berlin with my parents and sister.
2 My grandparents .... with us.
3 We .... a really good time.
4 We .... very nice food.
5 Mum .... lots of photos.
6 We .... interesting buildings and famous museums.
7 We .... bikes around the city.
8 My parents .... me some money.
9 I .... some postcards and a T-shirt.

5 Read the questions and choose the right answer.

0 Could you swim in the sea?
  a We could see.
  (b) Yes, we could.
1 Where did Holly and Alba go last weekend?
  a They went to the beach.
  b They go to the beach.
2 Did you enjoy your holiday?
  a Yes, we did.
  b Yes, we enjoyed.
3 Could Mehmet see the sea from his hotel room?
  a No, he can't.
  b No, he couldn't.
4 What did you eat last night?
  a We ate fish.
  b We eat fish.
5 Did Paola go to the park at the weekend?
  a Yes, she went.
  b Yes, she did.

6 👁 Students often make mistakes with verbs in the past simple. Correct the mistakes in these sentences.

1 I did a big party at my house with some music.
....
2 Last week my mum cook a really nice meal for me.
....
3 The weather was too hot. I don't want to go out.
....
4 One of my friends given me a great present.
....
5 I forgot my jacket in your house yesterday.
....

VOCABULARY

7 Read the sentences about a trip. Choose the best word (A, B, or C) for each space.

Example:
0 Last month I ....A.... to a big city for the weekend with my sister.
  A went   B stayed   C visited
1 We .... a really good time there.
  A did   B made   C had
2 We stayed at a .... hotel near the river.
  A fresh   B new   C young
3 On Saturday we .... in the beautiful park.
  A saw   B walked   C turned
4 We .... took photos of the cathedral.
  A also   B too   C more
5 On Sunday we went to .... of interesting museums.
  A many   B every   C lots

WRITING

8 Now write about a trip that you made.

....
....
....
....
....
....
....
....
....
....

The journey took nine months

VOCABULARY

1 Look at the pictures and write the words in the crossword.

Down

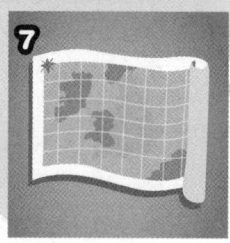

Across

LISTENING

2 ▶9 Listen to the conversation between Paul and Rebecca. Who says what? Write *P* for Paul and *R* for *Rebecca*.

0 How was your holiday? .....R.....
1 I went to Spain too! ....
2 We were there at the same time! ....
3 Who did you go with? ....
4 Where did you stay? ....
5 I love Spanish food. We had it every day. ....

3 ▶9 Listen again and answer the questions.

1 How long did Paul stay in Spain?
....
2 How long did Rebecca stay in Spain?
....
3 Who did Paul go to Spain with?
....
4 Who did Rebecca go with?
....
5 Where did Rebecca stay?
....

34 Unit 7

READING

4 Read the article and complete the table.

A WORLD OF ADVENTURE

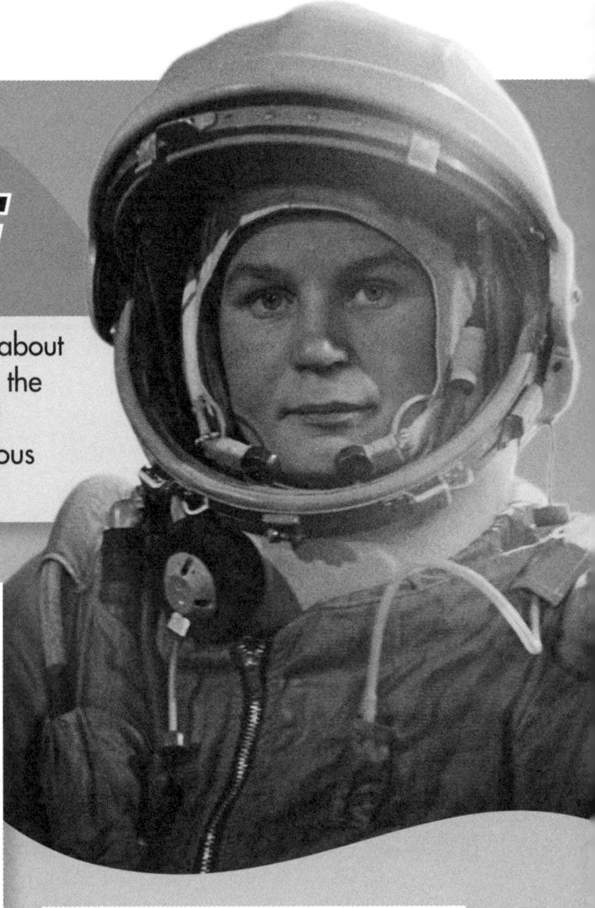

Today many people travel around the world. We know so much about places that are far away. Our world is smaller than it was. But in the past adventurers, explorers and travellers went to places and did things for the very first time. Read on to find out about three famous adventurers from history.

1 Ibn Battuta was born in Morocco in North Africa in 1304. He studied a lot and learned many things. He left home when he was a young man and travelled for almost thirty years. He went to three continents and visited many famous cities, such as Baghdad and Constantinople. We don't know exactly when he died, but some people say it was in 1377.

2 Ferdinand Magellan was born in Portugal in 1480. His parents were rich, but they died when Magellan was a boy. He became a sailor in 1505 and travelled to Africa and India. He was the first man from Europe to cross the Pacific Ocean. He died in 1521.

3 Valentina Tereshkova was born in a village in Russia in 1937. She was the first woman to go into space. She spent two days in space in June 1963. She was the fifth person from Russia to go into space. Before she became a cosmonaut she worked in a factory.

What was his/her name?	(1)	(3)	Valentina Tereshkova
Where was he/she born?	Morocco	Portugal	(5) ....
When was he/she born?	(2)	1480	(6) ....
Where did he/she go?	Baghdad, Constantinople	(4)	(7) ....

5 Read the article again and answer the questions.

1 How many years did Ibn Battuta travel?

....

2 How many continents did Ibn Battuta go to?

....

3 What did Ferdinand Magellan do for the first time?

....

4 When did Ferdinand Magellan die?

....

5 What did Valentina Tereshkova do for the first time?

....

6 Where did Valentina Tereshkova work before she became a cosmonaut?

....

8 Special places
Roald Dahl's room

VOCABULARY

1 Look at the pictures and write the words.

> armchair   carpet   cupboard   curtains   drawers   drawing   lamp   photographs   shelf

1 .... 2 .... 3 .... 4 .... 5 ....

   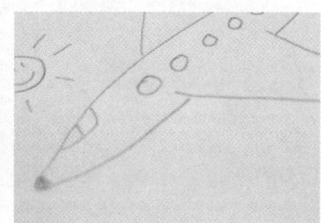

6 .... 7 .... 8 .... 9 ....

2 Match the texts to the pictures.

1 My special place is my computer room. It's got two windows with long curtains, a big armchair and lots of shelves with all my video games. I love it! I play computer games there every day after school.

2 My special place? Easy. That's my tree house. I keep all my favourite things there. I've also got lots of my drawings on the walls and a photograph of my friends on one of the shelves.

3 When I want to be alone, I go to my hut in the garden. It's my special place. I go there to read. I don't have an armchair there, so I sit on the floor on the carpet. It's very comfortable. My favourite thing in my special place is my lamp. It's very old and beautiful.

a    b    c

GRAMMAR someone, anyone, etc.

3 Match the two halves of the sentences.

1 Do you remember
2 There's nothing
3 Is there anywhere
4 I want to go
5 Can I have
6 No-one told me
7 Did anyone
8 Someone

a something to drink, please?
b that you liked tennis.
c anything about our maths homework?
d on TV tonight.
e somewhere quiet to read.
f we can go on Saturday?
g gave me flowers for my birthday.
h see that great film on TV last night?

4 Choose the right word to complete the sentences.

1 *Anyone* / *No-one* could answer the question.
2 There wasn't *anything* / *anyone* in the cupboard.
3 I had *nothing* / *anything* to do yesterday.
4 I want to go *someone* / *somewhere* interesting for my holidays.
5 Did *anyone* / *anywhere* pass the maths exam?

5 👁 Students often make mistakes with pronouns. <u>Underline</u> the mistakes in these sentences.

1 Some one gave me a T-shirt.

2 You don't have to bring nothing.

3 I don't have nothing to do, so we can go in the afternoon.

4 Can you tell me some thing about it?

6 Now write the sentences in Exercise 5 with the correct pronouns.

1 ....
2 ....
3 ....
4 ....

LISTENING

7 ▶10 Listen and choose the right answer.

1 People .... read KJ Neal's books.
  a in Europe   b all over the world.
2 KJ writes books for ....
  a children   b adults
3 KJ is .... years old.
  a fourteen   b thirteen
4 Her .... is her favourite place.
  a bedroom   b writing room
5 KJ's favourite thing is her ....
  a lamp   b armchair

8 ▶10 Listen to the interview again. Are the sentences right (✓) or wrong (✗)?

1 KJ's birthday is in January.   ....
2 She's from Scotland.   ....
3 She sometimes writes in her bedroom. ....
4 Her writing room is very big.   ....
5 Her bedroom is very small.   ....

Special places

My special place is the beach

VOCABULARY

1 Put the letters in the right order to make verbs and nouns.

1 n d i w ....
2 l n e t s i ....
3 m o c t u p r e ....
4 w d a r ....
5 e i w t r ....
6 s d r m u ....
7 d e r a ....

2 Complete the text with the words from Exercise 1.

In my house there is a lot of noise – my brother plays (1) .... games, my mum listens to the radio, my father plays the guitar, my sister plays the (2) .... That is why I go to my special place. I go to the top of the hill near my home and (3) .... to the sound of the (4) .... But that isn't the only thing I do there. I also go to my special place to (5) .... pictures, (6) .... magazines or (7) .... stories in my diary. I like to be on top of the hill. My special place is very important to me. Do you have somewhere that you go to?

READING

3 Complete the telephone conversation between two friends. What does Jonny say to Owen? Write the correct letter A–H in the space.

Example:
Owen: Hi, Jonny. It's Owen. How are you?
Jonny: 0 ...H...
Owen: Yes, I'm fine. Look, what are you doing tomorrow?
Jonny: 1 ....
Owen: Can you help me?
Jonny: 2 ....
Owen: Paint my bedroom with me. Can you come round?
Jonny: 3 ....
Owen: Great! But not until the afternoon, OK? I need to buy some paint first.
Jonny: 4 ....
Owen: Yes, that's fine.
Jonny: 5 ....
Owen: Brilliant! See you tomorrow, Jonny.

A That's OK.
B Maybe we can go there.
C Nothing special. Why's that?
D See you tomorrow then.
E Sure. What can I do?
F Yes, of course!
G OK. Shall we meet at two o'clock?
H Fine, thanks. You?

Prepare to write

4 Choose the right word to complete the sentences.

1 I don't like big cities *because* / *so* there are too many people.
2 My sister was very tired, *because* / *so* she stayed at home.
3 I only wore a T-shirt *because* / *so* it was very hot.
4 I couldn't go to the match *because* / *so* I had lots of homework.
5 My sister wants to swim in the Olympics, *because* / *so* she swims every day.
6 It rained all day, *because* / *so* we stayed at home.

5 Complete the text with *because* and *so*.

Somewhere I'd like to live

I'd like to live in New York (1) .... I think it's an interesting place. I went to the city on holiday last year and I loved it. When I was there, I visited the Statue of Liberty, Brooklyn Bridge and Ellis Island. I also went to Central Park (2) .... I wanted to go running there. I really like big cities, (3) .... New York is the place for me!

6 Now write about somewhere you'd like to live.

9 Clothes and fashion
Those shoes are yours

VOCABULARY

1 Look at the pictures and write the words.

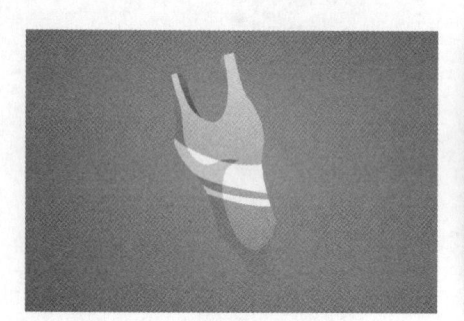

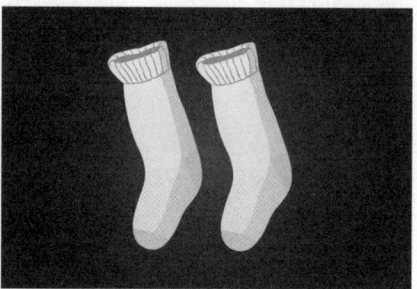

1 .... 2 .... 3 ....

4 .... 5 .... 6 ....

2 Read the sentences and write the words from Exercise 1.

1 You wear this at the beach.
....

2 You wear these on your feet.
....

3 You wear these on your legs when you do sports.
....

4 You wear this on your head.
....

5 When it's cold, you wear this.
....

6 This usually has pockets.
....

3 Put the words in the right order to make sentences and questions.

1 jumper / red / my / is / favourite
....

2 cap / this / like / you / do
.... ?

3 this / want / jacket / buy / I / to
....

4 green / wearing / you / are / why / socks
.... ?

5 are / football / blue / my / shorts
....

6 swimming / costume / my / where / is
.... ?

GRAMMAR Pronouns and determiners

4 Match the sentences.

1 It's my pen.   a It's yours.
2 It's your phone.   b They're hers.
3 They're his books.   c They're theirs.
4 They're our video games. d It's mine.
5 They're her pencils.   e They're his.
6 They're their bags.   f They're ours.

5 Look at the words in brackets. Write determiners.

0 This is my bike and that's ...his... (Colin's bike).
1 This isn't Clara's book. Isn't that .... (Clara's book)?
2 I've got your mobile, but I can't find .... (my mobile).
3 This is my bag. Where's .... (your bag)?
4 That is your computer and this is .... (our computer).
5 These are our tickets and those are .... (Federico and Marta's tickets).

6 👁 Students often make mistakes with determiners. Correct the mistakes in these sentences. Two of the sentences are correct.

1 Please could you bring it to me house?
....
2 Last week I moved my house.
....
3 Thank you for writing.
....
4 I bought it because I love his design.
....
5 See you at your party.
....

READING

7 Read the article and answer the questions.

1 Who does Bella make clothes for?
....
2 Where is Rocco Canal from?
....
3 Which fashion shows does Bella go to?
....
4 What is Bella's favourite place?
....
5 Where does she live for most of the year?
....

8 Read the article again. Choose the right word (a or b) for each space.

0 Bella doesn't make clothes for ...b... .
   a actors   b sports stars
1 Bella doesn't make ....
   a caps   b jackets
2 Bella's hats are ....
   a cheap   b expensive
3 Bella wants to have .... lessons.
   a French   b Italian
4 Bella goes to .... in December.
   a New York   b Paris
5 Bella doesn't like New York when it ....
   a rains   b snows

Bella McCarthy is famous all over the world. She makes clothes for actors, dancers and singers but she doesn't make clothes for sports stars because she isn't interested in sport. Bella makes hats, jumpers and jackets but she doesn't make shoes or caps. 'I don't like caps,' she says. 'They are for football coaches and men with no hair.'

People love buying jackets or jumpers with the special BM label on them. But the clothes aren't cheap. 'I don't want to pay £199 for one of Bella's hats,' says Italian fashion designer Rocco Canal. 'I can get a good one for only £20!'

Every year Bella goes to fashion shows in London, Milan, Paris and New York. Her favourite place is Paris because she loves French food. Bella speaks Italian very well but she doesn't speak French. 'I'm going to have lessons,' she says. 'I hope I can find the time!'

Bella lives in London for most of the year but she spends every Christmas in New York. 'It's the best place to be in December,' she says. 'I love New York when it snows, but I don't like it in the rain!'

Clothes and fashion

Is your jumper made of cheese?

VOCABULARY

1 Put the letters in order to make clothes words.

1 s c i t l a p ....
2 r a t h e e l ....
3 n o t c o t ....
4 l o w o ....

2 Now complete the text with words from Exercise 1.

I love clothes! They are my favourite things. I go shopping for clothes with my friends every Saturday. Last Saturday, I bought a jumper made of (1) .... Sara bought a T-shirt made of (2) .... and a pair of (3) .... shoes. Jake bought a pair of black sunglasses. They are made of (4) ....

3 Circle the right word to complete the sentences.

1 Socks aren't made of *cotton* / *plastic*.
2 Footballs aren't made of *plastic* / *wool*.
3 Water bottles aren't made of *leather* / *plastic*.
4 Computers aren't made of *plastic* / *cotton*.

LISTENING

4 ▶11 You will hear five short conversations. There is one question for each conversation. For each question, choose the right answer (A, B or C).

Example:
0 Which is the boy's cap?
A ☐ B ✓ C ☐

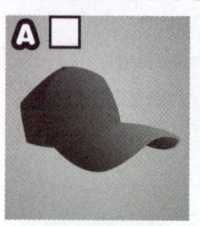

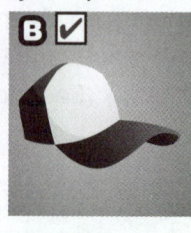

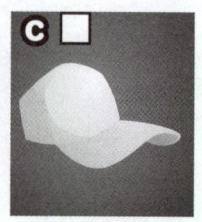

1 What did Janet buy?
A ☐ B ☐ C ☐

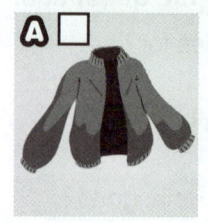

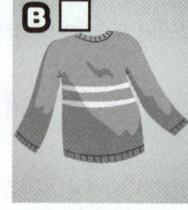

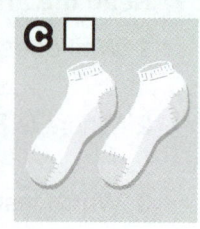

2 When does the football match start?
A ☐ B ☐ C ☐

3 Where did the boy go?
A ☐ B ☐ C ☐

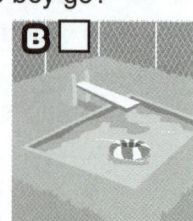

4 How many children went to the cinema?
A ☐ 2 B ☐ 3 C ☐ 4

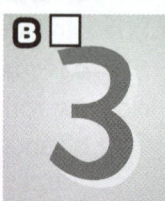

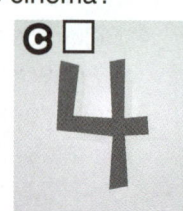

5 How much did the boy pay for the jacket?
A ☐ £20 B ☐ £30 C ☐ £50

WRITING

5 Complete the texts with the words in the boxes.

`made   paper   rains   wear`

`dad   leather   most   paper`

My favourite clothes

The thing I wear most is my leather jacket. I love it! My parents gave it to me for my birthday last year. I (1) .... it every day. My friend Richard thinks that leather jackets are really boring. He thinks they are for old rock stars and history teachers. His jacket is (2) .... of (3) .... He thinks his jacket is very cool, but it's not very good when it (4) ....

My favourite clothes

The thing I love (5) .... is my jacket. I made it myself from (6) .... My friend Tim doesn't like my jacket very much. He prefers his (7) .... one. Tim thinks he looks very cool in his jacket, but I think he looks like my (8) ....

6 Read the texts again and answer the questions.

1 Who has a jacket made of leather?
....

2 Who has a jacket made of paper?
....

3 Who gave Tim his jacket?
....

4 Who made Richard's jacket?
....

7 Now write about your favourite clothes. Describe what they are made of.

....
....
....
....
....
....
....

Clothes and fashion   43

10 Buying things
Are the sunglasses in the sale?

VOCABULARY

1 Find ten shopping words.

s	h	o	p	p	i	n	g	c	e	n	t	r	e
p	m	e	z	m	a	k	e	-	u	p	l	f	h
e	x	p	e	n	s	i	v	e	g	s	w	j	o
n	a	w	u	m	a	r	k	e	t	a	a	e	j
d	y	d	r	r	m	p	g	x	n	g	s	l	v
i	r	z	t	o	s	u	x	n	p	t	i	u	e
w	a	l	l	e	t	e	a	c	h	i	g	a	b
s	h	o	p	a	s	s	i	s	t	a	n	t	p

2 Complete the sentences with words from Exercise 1.

1 My sister got some .... in the sale.

2 Tom lost his .... in the shop.

3 I bought my mother a .... for her birthday.

4 A new .... opened in our town last week. Everything was half price in the shops!

5 We couldn't see the .... for the jewellery department.

6 The .... helped me find the earrings. He was very friendly!

GRAMMAR *some, any, a bit of, a few, a lot of*

3 Put the words in the right order to make sentences and questions.

1 there / a / people / café / the / lot / were / of / in
   ....
2 for / my / birthday / books / some / I / would / like
   ....
3 any / have / you / do / money
   .... ?
4 games / any / video / got / brother / hasn't / my
   ....
5 DVDs / few / a / got / my / parents / have
   ....
6 cake / bit / of / a / you / like / would
   .... ?

4 Choose the right word or phrase to complete the sentences.

1 My brother has got *a lot of* / *any* friends on Facebook.
2 We've only got *a few* / *a bit of* packets of crisps in the cupboard.
3 My friends haven't got *some* / *any* pets.
4 Do you have *a bit of* / *a few* time to help me with my homework?
5 My sister bought *any* / *some* new sunglasses.
6 I've got *a lot of* / *a few* books. I counted them yesterday. I've got 854!

5 👁 Students often make mistakes with *some, any, a bit of, a few, a lot of*. Correct the mistakes in these sentences.

1 You need to bring a paper and a pencil.
   ....
2 There isn't a any water in the flat.
   ....
3 I like it because I don't have any TV in my room.
   ....
4 Please, wear some old shirt and old trousers.
   ....
5 They cost very much.
   ....

WRITING

6 Complete Stefani's blog. Write ONE word for each space.

Example: | **0** | *is* |

My brother's name **(0)** .... Justin. He is two years older **(1)** .... me and he really enjoys shopping. **(2)** .... goes to **(3)** .... shopping centre near our house twice **(4)** .... week. He goes there **(5)** .... his friends. They stay for hours and look in every shop.

Justin doesn't always buy things at the shopping centre, **(6)** .... last Saturday he spent all **(7)** .... birthday money. He bought some video games, a pair **(8)** .... sunglasses and a **(9)** .... books. Justin often asks me to **(10)** .... shopping with him, but I'm not interested.

Buying things

Buying and selling online

LISTENING

1 ▶12 Listen to the description of World of Shopping. Match the shops to the floors.

1 Salsa	a Floor 4
2 The Film House	b Floor 2
3 The Ring Shop	c Floor 10
4 Harry James	d Floor 3
5 Money, Money, Money	e Floor 7
6 Face Paint	f Floor 9

2 ▶12 Listen again. Are the sentences right (✔) or wrong (✘)?

1 Salsa is a shop. ....
2 The shopping centre has 50 floors. ....
3 The Film House is a cinema. ....
4 The Ring Shop and Harry James sell jewellery. ....
5 You can buy wallets and purses in Face Paint. ....

3 ▶12 Listen again. Complete the sentences from the description. Use the words in the box.

> always   are   favourite   great   hungry   need

1 Welcome to World of Shopping, your .... shopping centre.
2 It's .... summer in here.
3 Are you .... ?
4 I have .... news for all you jewellery lovers.
5 Do you .... a new wallet or purse?
6 You .... at the right place.

46 Unit 10

Prepare to write

4 Read the article and number the sentences in the right order.

Robert was a young entrepreneur. He started a company online called the News Company. The News Company sold stories about famous actors, singers and TV stars. At first, people didn't want to buy stories online about famous actors, singers and TV stars. 'We can get them for free on other websites,' they said. Robert wasn't very happy about that.

Then he had a great idea. He asked people to sell their own stories about famous actors, singers and TV stars on The News Company's website. Robert wanted 50% of the money that people made.

Three months after that, people started buying and selling lots of stories on The News Company website. Robert made lots of money. He was very happy about that.

Two years later Robert sold The News Company to a bigger company called The Bigger News Company. But he was sad about that.

Finally, he started a new company online called The Much Bigger News Company. The Much Bigger News Company bought The Bigger News Company and Robert's website was suddenly the most important website in the world. Robert was very happy about that.

- **a** Robert bought his old company. ....
- **b** The company didn't do very well. ....
- **c** Robert sold the company. ....
- **d** Robert made a lot of money. ....
- **e** Robert started a company. ......1.....
- **f** Robert started a new company. ....
- **g** Robert had a great idea. ....

5 Now write your own article about a young internet entrepreneur. Use *then, after that, later, finally*.

11 Eating out
Which restaurant is better?

VOCABULARY

1 Find the odd one out.

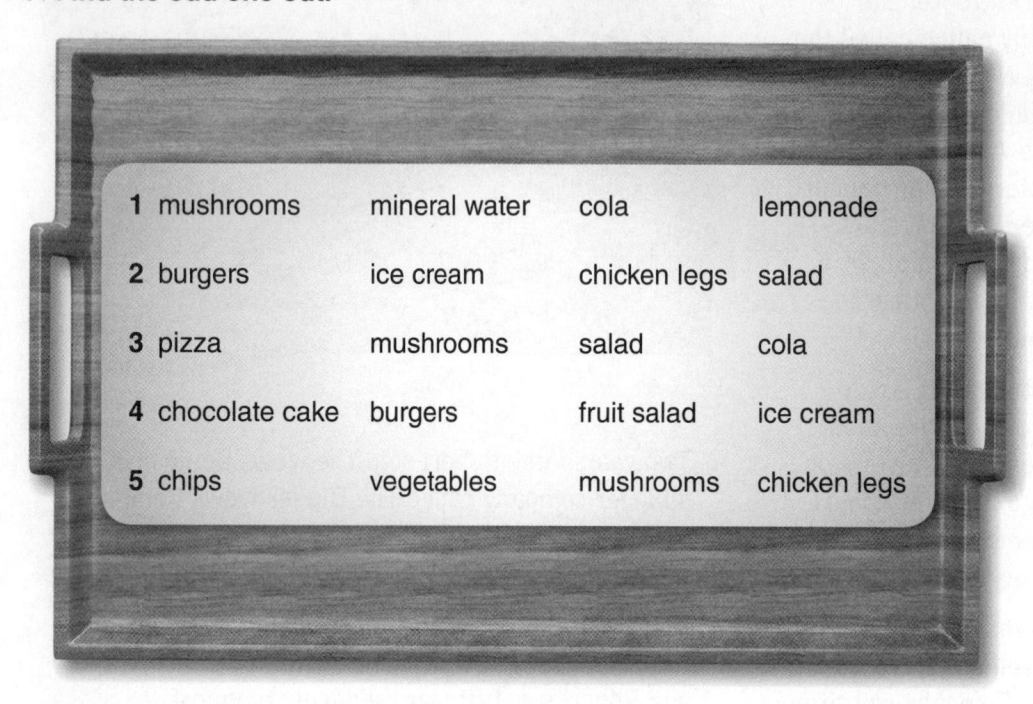

1	mushrooms	mineral water	cola	lemonade
2	burgers	ice cream	chicken legs	salad
3	pizza	mushrooms	salad	cola
4	chocolate cake	burgers	fruit salad	ice cream
5	chips	vegetables	mushrooms	chicken legs

GRAMMAR *as … as*

2 Complete the sentences with *as … as*.

1 Richard is .... (old) Simon.
2 Edinburgh is .... (not big) London.
3 My sister is .... (funny) yours.
4 The new Batman films are .... (not interesting) the old ones.
5 Is your new video game .... (exciting) mine?
6 I'm .... (not tall) my father.

Comparative adjectives

3 Write the comparative adjectives.

1 cold   ....
2 hot   ....
3 short   ....
4 popular   ....
5 busy   ....

4 Now complete the sentences with the comparative adjectives from Exercise 3.

1 Football is a .... sport than tennis in most countries.
2 It's .... in the south of Italy than in the south of England.
3 Life in big cities is .... than it is in small towns. Everyone is always running from place to place in Buenos Aires, Moscow and Warsaw.
4 I'm .... than my sister. She's so tall!
5 Scotland in winter is .... than Spain.

5 👁 **Students often make mistakes with comparative adjectives. Correct the mistakes in these sentences. Two of the sentences are correct.**

1 I hope you are well than before.
....
2 My brother is younger than me.
....
3 Yesterday I went shopping with my old sister.
....
4 It's interesting and biggest than the others.
....
5 My new room is smaller than my old room.
....

LISTENING

6 ▶13 **You will hear a boy asking a friend about a pizza-making class. Listen and complete Michael's notes.**

Pizza-making class

Day: ......Wednesday......
Teacher's name: (1) Sally ....
Price for one class: (2) £ ....
Place: (3) in the .... in Old Street.
Teacher's website: (4) www...............................com
Start time: (5) ....

Street food

VOCABULARY

1 Put the letters in order to make food words.

1. a t e m ....
2. s o n i n o ....
3. a p c e k n a ....
4. s e o t t m o a ....
5. o u m r o s h m ....
6. p s u o ....
7. e l m t e o e t ....
8. e c i r ....
9. s e l o n o d ....
10. a s n n a b a ....
11. s s s g a e a u ....
12. o o f e a s d ....

3 Read the email again and answer the questions.

1. Why did Leonardo go to the restaurant?
....
2. Where is the restaurant?
....
3. Were there many people at the restaurant?
....
4. Who had fruit salad and cream for dessert?
....
5. How much did Leonardo's parents pay for the meal?
....

READING

2 Look at the pictures. Complete the email with the words.

Hi Sarah,

I had a great day yesterday! It was my fourteenth birthday and my parents took me to the new American restaurant in our town. Do you know it, Sarah? It's next to the cinema. I had (0) ......burgers...... and (1) .... for my main course and I drank a glass of (2) .... that was made with fresh lemons! My mother had an omelette and a (3) .... and my father had grilled (4) .... The restaurant is very popular. It was so busy! We had to wait to get our food, but that was OK. Everyone was very friendly and there was a band playing music!

The best part of the meal was dessert. I had chocolate (5) .... My mum had fruit salad and cream, but Dad didn't have anything. At the end of the meal, the manager came over to our table. 'Happy birthday, young man,' he said. 'Would you like your present now?' Do you know what my present was, Sarah? The meal! My parents didn't have to pay for it! We were all very surprised.

Email soon!

Love,

Leonardo

WRITING

4 Match the questions to the answers.

1 What is the restaurant called?
2 Where is the restaurant?
3 What kind of food can you eat there?
4 What did you eat at the restaurant?
5 What did you think of the restaurant?

a You can eat Italian food there.
b The food is great and the waiters are friendly. I really liked it!
c It's in the centre of town, next to the new shopping centre.
d The restaurant is called Ciao.
e I ate a mushroom pizza. It was very good!

5 Now write a review of the restaurant. Use the answers to the questions in Exercise 4.

The restaurant is called Ciao.

6 Now write a review of a restaurant that you know. Answer the questions in Exercise 4.

12 The latest technology
Supercomputers

VOCABULARY

1 Find six technology words.

d	o	w	n	l	o	a	d
i	m	a	c	h	i	n	e
g	o	e	f	u	p	q	a
i	s	t	m	i	m	v	j
t	x	t	l	o	w	u	e
a	r	u	a	y	r	l	o
l	z	a	e	r	b	y	h
m	v	i	r	u	s	e	s

2 Complete the sentences with the words from Exercise 1.

1 Scientists can study the .... using the latest technology.
2 Computer .... are a problem on the internet.
3 .... computers are getting faster and faster.
4 The first computer was a counting ....
5 It doesn't take long to .... a document from the internet.
6 The .... is the part of the computer where information is kept.

GRAMMAR Superlative adjectives

3 Write the superlative adjectives.

1 better   ....
2 worse   ....
3 quicker   ....
4 exciting   ....
5 heavier   ....
6 famous   ....
7 clever   ....
8 thin   ....

4 Match the two halves of the sentences.

1 Rome is one of the oldest
2 São Paulo is the
3 London is the most
4 Paris is one of the most
5 San Francisco is the
6 Madrid is the highest

a beautiful cities in Europe.
b expensive city in England.
c cities in the world.
d friendliest city in the USA.
e capital city in Europe.
f biggest city in South America.

52 Unit 12

5 Put the words in the right order to make two different sentences.

0 river / longest / the / in / Nile / world / the / is / the
The Nile is the longest river in the world.
The longest river in the world is the Nile.

1 the / footballer / in / exciting / league / the / Messi / Spanish / is / most
....
....
....

2 Lady Gaga / one / most / on / popular / Twitter / people / is / of / the
....
....
....

3 scientists / Marie Curie / cleverest / history / the / one / was / of / in
....
....
....

4 one / the / world / is / the / Buenos Aires / of / beautiful / cities / most / in
....
....
....

6 ⊙ Students often make mistakes with superlatives. Correct the mistakes in these sentences.

1 It was the great holiday ever.
....

2 You should go to the Metro Centre because it's the big shopping centre in the world.
....

3 You can wear your older clothes for this job.
....

4 I'm really happy that you are coming tomorrow and it's better you come at 7 pm.
....

5 The most expensive cost £900 and the cheaper cost £400.
....

READING

7 Complete the conversation with the words in the box.

| better | fun | prefer | right |
| sounds | turn | type | week |

Mr Howe: Good morning, everyone. Now what did we do in our technology class last (1) .... ?

Peter: We downloaded information from the internet.

Mr Howe: Ah, yes, that's (2) .... Now today we're going to write a computer program.

Jane: That (3) .... difficult!

Peter: No, it isn't. My brother has written lots of programs. It's easy!

Mr Howe: We're going to write a games program.

Jane: I like computer games. That'll be (4) .... !

Mr Howe: What (5) .... of game would you like to write?

Peter: Can we write a football game?

Jane: I don't like football. I (6) .... adventure games.

Mr Howe: What about a car racing game?

Jane: OK, that's (7) .... than football!

Mr Howe: Good. Let's start. So, (8) .... on your computers.

The latest technology 53

Me and my computer

VOCABULARY

1 Match the sentences to the words.

1. This is a machine that makes pictures or writing on paper.
2. This is a small computer that you can carry around.
3. Every computer has this and there are letters, numbers and other things on it.
4. This is the part of a computer that sound comes out of.
5. Pictures and words are shown on this on a computer.
6. This is a small object that you move with your hand to make a computer do different things.

a laptop
b screen
c speaker
d keyboard
e mouse
f printer

2 What can you do online? Complete the table with these nouns.

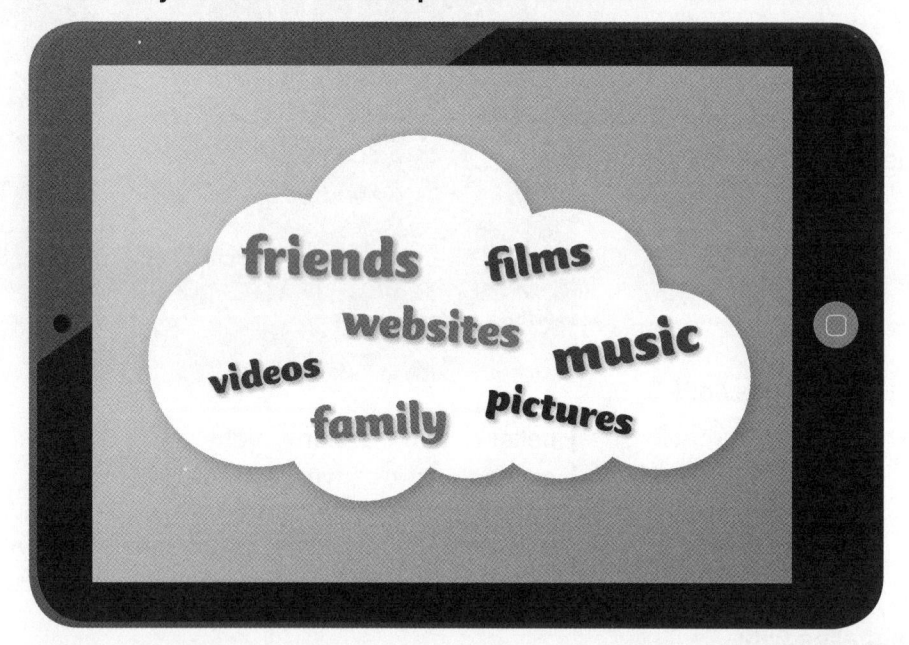

friends   films   websites   videos   music   family   pictures

visit	chat to	watch	download
......	......	......	......

LISTENING

3 ▶14 Listen to Tom talking to Liz about going to a Technology festival. For each question, choose the right answer (A, B or C).

Example:

0 Who is going to the festival with Tom?
  A Rachel
  B John
  C Chris

1 The festival is
  A in the library.
  B in the sports centre.
  C in the park.

2 One ticket will cost
  A £8.
  B £10.
  C £15.

3 They will meet
  A at the bus station.
  B at the café.
  C at the park.

4 What food can people buy at the festival?
  A sandwiches
  B pizza
  C cake

5 The festival will finish at
  A 5.00
  B 6.00
  C 7.00

54 Unit 12

Prepare to write

4 Complete the email with the words in the box.

> digital   email   hi   laptops   printer   wishes

(1) .... Colin,

I went to the technology festival with Tom and Rachel on Sunday. It was great! There were lots of things there. We saw the latest (2) .... They were different to the usual ones. They all had touch screens!

Tom's favourite thing at the festival was a very small (3) .... camera. Rachel liked the 3D (4) .... It printed a violin and you could play it! Can you believe that?

Send me an (5) .... soon!

Best (6) .... ,

Liz

5 Read the email again and answer the questions.

1 Where did Liz go?
   ....
2 Why were the laptops different?
   ....
3 What was Tom's favourite thing?
   ....
4 What did Rachel like?
   ....

6 Now write an email to a friend. Write about one of these things.

a Your favourite website
b The last video game you played
c Your favourite piece of technology (e.g. laptop, tablet, digital camera)

....
....
....
....
....
....
....
....

The latest technology   55

13 Healthy bodies
What's the matter?

VOCABULARY

1 Put the letters in the right order to make health words.

1 l d o c ....
2 p m e t a e r r u t e ....
3 n p i a ....
4 d c e h a a e h ....
5 n k e r b o ....
6 m o a h c t s   h e c a ....
7 o t o c a t h h e ....
8 t h u r ....
9 c i k s ....

2 Complete the sentences with words from Exercise 1.

1 I can't play tennis today because I feel ....

2 A: Are you OK?
 B: No, I don't feel very well. My ears ....

3 The dentist said my .... will be better soon.

4 A: What's wrong?
 B: I've got a .... in my leg.

5 37.5? You have a very high ....

GRAMMAR should/shouldn't

3 Choose the right word to complete the sentences.

To be healthy …
1 You *should* / *shouldn't* sleep seven or eight hours every night.
2 You *should* / *shouldn't* drink lots of water.
3 You *should* / *shouldn't* go to bed late.
4 You *should* / *shouldn't* exercise four or five times a week.
5 You *should* / *shouldn't* eat too much chocolate or cake.
6 You *should* / *shouldn't* eat lots of fish, fruit and vegetables.

4 Complete the sentences with the phrases in the box.

> drink lots of water   eat so much chocolate
> go to bed   play tennis this afternoon
> sit down   study hard tonight

1 A: I've got a pain in my right arm.
  B: You shouldn't .... then.
2 A: I'm very tired.
  B: Then you should ...., Sam.
3 A: My foot hurts.
  B: You should .... for a while.
4 A: I feel sick.
  B: Well, you shouldn't .... !
5 A: I've got a difficult maths exam tomorrow.
  B: You should .... then.
6 A: Sarah's got a terrible cold.
  B: She should rest and ....

5 Read the sentences. Which advice is good and which is bad?

To improve your English
0 You should study every day.
   ....good....
1 You should read books in English.
   ....
2 You shouldn't talk to people from English-speaking countries.
   ....
3 You should listen to music in English.
   ....
4 You shouldn't watch films in English.
   ....
5 You shouldn't practise pronunciation.
   ....

6 Students often make mistakes with should/shouldn't. Correct the mistakes in these sentences. Two of the sentences are correct.

1 Don't worry about what should you wear.
  ....
2 I should bring a DVD?
  ....
3 How much money should we bring?
  ....
4 You shouldn't eat sweets when you feel sick.
  ....
5 I can't decide what colour should I paint it.
  ....

LISTENING

7 ▶15 Listen to five short conversations. Are the sentences right (✓) or wrong (✗)?

1 William hasn't got a headache.   ....
2 Susie has got a pain in her arm.   ....
3 Carla's eye hurts.   ....
4 Marek thinks his hand is broken.   ....
5 Javi feels better.   ....

8 ▶15 Listen again. Complete the sentences from the conversations. Use the words in the box.

> broken   headache   matter   medicine   wrong

1 You should take some ....
2 What's the ...., Susie?
3 What's ...., Carla?
4 I think it's ....
5 What about your .... ?

Healthy bodies

You should enter the race!

VOCABULARY

1 Complete the blog with the words in the box.

> advice   enter   finish
> get   kilometres   well

FITNESS FOR EVERYONE

Hi, everyone. Today I've got some great (1) .... for people who want to start running. Read on for my top eight tips!

- Eat (2) ....
- Get lots of rest.
- Drink lots of water.
- Start slowly.
- Run five times a week.
- Remember it feels great to (3) .... fit.
- Tell yourself, 'I'm going to run five (4) .... before the end of the summer.'
- (5) .... a race when you are ready. And always (6) .... the races that you enter!

2 Match the two halves of the sentences.

1. It is very
2. I got fit by cycling,
3. Swimming
4. Some people think

a. exercise is boring.
b. swimming and running.
c. is good exercise.
d. important to exercise.

READING

3 Read the article. Choose the right word (a or b) for each space.

My cousin Alex runs three (1) .... every morning before school, she cycles to school, she swims in the school swimming pool at lunchtime, and then she cycles home after school. Can you believe (2) .... ?

On Saturdays she enters (3) .... These are special events called 'triathlons'. In triathlons, the athletes have to swim, cycle and run a very long way. Alex is very (4) .... at triathlons. Last year, she won six events, finished second three times, and third four times. Alex wants to be in the Olympics when she is older.

Alex has lots of good advice for people who want to (5) .... fit. 'Don't think about it, don't talk about it, just do it. Oh, and don't do (6) .... exercise on Sundays. Have a rest that day. I always do. It's very important to have a rest.'

1	a kilometre	b	kilometres
2	a them	b	it
3	a races	b	race
4	a good	b	well
5	a got	b	get
6	a any	b	some

4 Read the article again and answer the questions.

1 How does Alex get to school?
....
2 What does she do at lunchtime?
....
3 What does Alex do on Saturdays?
....
4 What does Alex want to do when she is older?
....
5 When does Alex have a rest?
....

WRITING

5 Read the email from your friend Sandra.

From:	Sandra
To:	

It's great you're feeling better. Where do you want to run tomorrow? What time shall we meet? Which race do you want to enter next weekend?

Write Sandra an email. Answer the questions. Write 25–35 words.

....
....
....
....
....
....

14 In the town
Turn right at the roundabout

VOCABULARY

1 Match the sentences to the words.

1 The colour of these changes from red and yellow to green when the traffic can go.
2 This is a large area of grass and trees in a city where children can play.
3 People and cars can use this to go across a river or a road.
4 This is round and is the place where several roads meet.
5 This is the word for something that has a roof and walls.

a roundabout
b traffic lights
c building
d park
e bridge

2 Complete the sentences with the words in the box.

> bridge   river   building
> street   park

1 Kensington Gardens is the name of a famous ....park.... in London.
2 The Champs-Elysées is a long .... in Paris.
3 The Amazon is a very long .... in South America.
4 The Pantheon is an ancient .... in Rome.
5 The Golden Gate is the name of a famous .... in San Francisco.

GRAMMAR Prepositions

3 Look at the map. Choose the right preposition to complete the sentences.

1 The museum is *next to / opposite* the park.
2 The train station is *next to / near* the football stadium.
3 There is a car park *outside / next to* the town.
4 The restaurant is *in front of / next to* the cinema.
5 The cinema is *opposite / between* the café and the restaurant.

4 Look at the map and complete the sentences.

1 The football stadium is .... the town.
2 The cinema is .... the café.
3 The restaurant is .... the post office.
4 The bank is .... the park.
5 There is a river going .... the town.
6 There is a bridge .... the river.
7 There is a market .... the shopping centre.
8 There is a car park .... the train station.

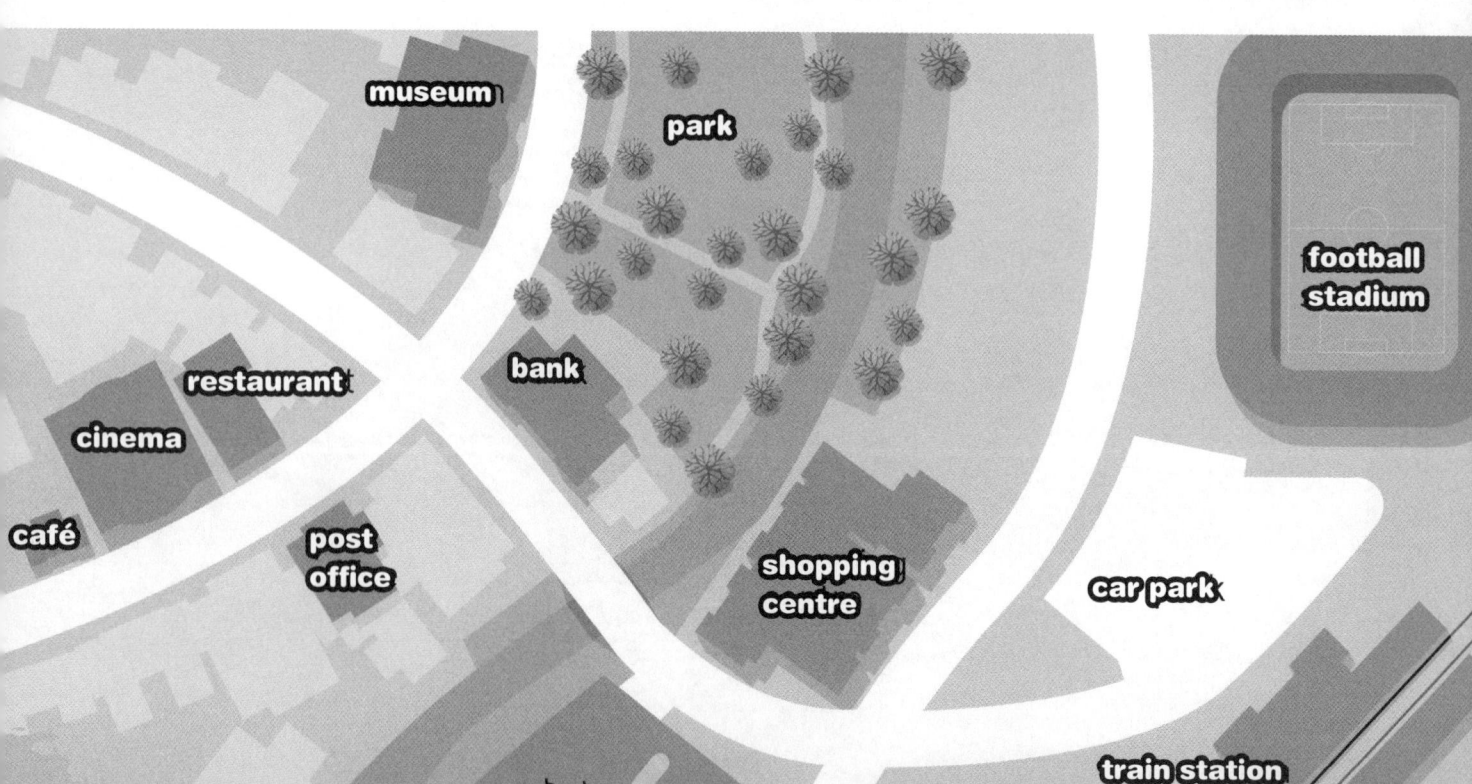

60 Unit 14

5 Complete the conversations with the words in the box.

go   near   on   turn   way   where

1 **Man:** Which (1) .... is the library?
  Woman: Go straight (2) .... The library is on your left.
2 **Girl:** Is there a post office (3) .... here?
  Boy: Yes, there is. (4) .... left at the roundabout. The post office is on your right.
3 **Boy:** Excuse me, (5) .... is the bank?
  Girl: It's opposite the cinema. (6) .... past the supermarket and it's on your left.

6 Students often make mistakes with prepositions. Correct the mistakes in these sentences. Two of the sentences are correct.

1 Every day she goes out side.

....

2 I live opposite the supermarket.

....

3 We can meet out of my house.

....

4 Go through the main street.

....

5 The lake has a bridge across it.

....

READING

7 Complete the text with prepositions.

My name is Clara and I'm (1) .... Sydney. I'm thirteen. I live (2) .... a small house (3) .... my parents, my sister, and my dog. Sydney is a big, noisy city, but we're very happy living here.

There's so much to do in Sydney. There are great museums, theatres and cinemas. There are lots of restaurants and cafés. If you like shopping, you'll find everything you need here. I don't like shopping, so I never go (4) .... Oxford Street in the centre (5) .... the city! But do you know my favourite thing about Sydney? It's the beaches! Some cities don't have any beaches, but Sydney has lots of them.

I often go to Manly Beach and Coogee Beach, but my favourite beach is Bondi. I go there with my family (6) .... sunny days. Bondi Beach is very big! We like playing beach volleyball there.

8 Read the text again. Are the sentences right (✔) or wrong (✘)?

1 Clara lives with her parents, her dog and her sister. ....
2 They like living in Sydney. ....
3 Clara doesn't like shopping. ....
4 She sometimes goes to Oxford Street. ....
5 Clara likes Sydney's beaches. ....
6 She usually goes to Coogee Beach. ....

A trip to Edinburgh

READING

1 Which notice (A–H) says this (1–5)? For questions 1–5, choose the correct letter A–H.

Example:

0 This shop is now in a different place. **E**

1 If you buy a snack this morning, we'll give you something extra. ☐

2 Parents don't need to pay for their children to go on this with them. ☐

3 This afternoon you can hear about the history of this place. ☐

4 There are hot things to eat here today. ☐

5 You can visit this website to choose something special to eat. ☐

A New café opening here soon! Information on our website: www.fqbookshop.abc

B MUSEUM CAFÉ — Soup and pasta available this lunchtime – just ask!

C Book chocolate factory tours HERE — ADULTS £5, KIDS FREE! NEXT TOUR 2.30 PM

D NICO'S PIZZAS — TWO FOR THE PRICE OF ONE NEXT MONDAY AND TUESDAY!

E Just John's is now opposite the market … and sells great sweets!

F CASTLE FOOD 1900–2000 — INTERESTING TALK IN THE OLD KITCHEN STARTS 3 PM

G FREE HOT OR COLD DRINK WITH YOUR SANDWICH BEFORE 12.30

H CONNIE'S CAKES — GO ONLINE TO SEE THE BIRTHDAY CAKES WE CAN MAKE: WWW.CONNIESCAKES.OZV

VOCABULARY

2 Match the words to make compound nouns.

1	bus	a	centre
2	town	b	office
3	walking	c	stop
4	post	d	station
5	bus	e	tour

3 Complete the text with the compound nouns from Exercise 2.

> Last summer I went to Italy on a
> (1) .... with my
> parents and my younger sister. It was
> great! We caught a bus from the
> large (2) .... in
> Bergamo (3) ....
> Two hours later the bus stopped at a
> (4) .... near a
> river. That was the start of our walk!
> We walked past lakes, through villages,
> and over mountains. It was very
> beautiful. In one village we found a very
> small (5) .... and
> bought some postcards to send home.

LISTENING

4 ▶16 Listen to Lucas talking to a friend about his trip to Cardiff with his family. What place did each person like the most? For questions 1–5, write a letter (A–H) next to each person.

Example:

0	Lucas	C	A	castle
1	Sister	☐	B	cinema
2	Brother	☐	C	clothes shop
3	Mum	☐	D	park
4	Dad	☐	E	museum
5	Grandfather	☐	F	restaurant
			G	theatre
			H	stadium

Prepare to write

5 Write *this* or *these*.

1 .... buildings
2 .... streets
3 .... river
4 .... park
5 .... museums
6 .... cinema

6 Choose the right words to complete the text.

> Budapest is the capital of Hungary and it's in the centre of Europe. (1) *This / These* city is one of the most beautiful in the world. The River Danube goes through the city. On one side of (2) *this / these* river there is the old part of the city. It is called Buda. There are many beautiful old buildings there. (3) *This / These* are very popular with tourists. On the other side is the new part of the city called Pest. There are lots of cinemas there. (4) *This / These* cinemas show lots of interesting films. Margaret Island is a very interesting place in Budapest. It's in the middle of the Danube in the centre of the city. (5) *This / These* island has parks, tennis courts and swimming pools.

7 Now write about your town or city. Use *this* and *these*.

....
....
....
....
....
....
....
....
....
....
....

In the town

15 Weather and places
It was snowing yesterday at 5 pm

VOCABULARY

1 Complete the table with the nouns.

Adjectives	Nouns
cloudy	cloud
foggy	....
sunny	....
snowy	....
rainy	....
windy	....

2 Complete the sentences with nouns and adjectives from Exercise 1.

1 I like going to the beach when it's su.................... .
2 Look at that big black cl.................... in the sky.
3 We had a lot of sn.................... last night. Let's go skiing!
4 It's so fo.................... . I can't see anything!
5 It's very ra.................... today. It isn't the best weather for playing football.

3 Complete the sentences with the words in the box.

| cold   like   temperature   thunderstorms   weather |

1 We had great .... on our holiday. It was sunny every day.
2 It was so .... last winter.
3 My dog doesn't like .... She's afraid of them.
4 What's the .... today? Is it hot?
5 What was the weather .... yesterday?

GRAMMAR Past continuous

4 Look at the picture and correct the sentences.

0 Mr and Mrs Dawson were eating pizza.
   They weren't eating pizza.
   They were making pizza.

1 Cathy was doing her homework.
   ....

2 Tony was playing the piano.
   ....

3 David was reading a magazine.
   ....

4 Cheryl and John were playing football.
   ....

5 Grandma Dawson was singing.
   ....

5 Write complete questions. Use the past continuous.

0 Mark / watch / TV last night
   Was Mark watching TV last night ?

1 he / help his parents
   .... ?

2 Tanya and Karl / swim in the sea
   .... ?

3 they / do their homework
   .... ?

4 your friend / play volleyball
   .... ?

5 you / read a book
   .... ?

6 Students often make mistakes with the past continuous. Correct the mistakes in these sentences. Two of the sentences are correct.

1 I was enjoying my birthday party last week.
   ....

2 What were you doing yesterday at 4 pm?
   ....

3 I went to the cinema yesterday.
   ....

4 I liked it because was playing my favourite team.
   ....

5 When we were on holiday, we were swimming every day.
   ....

LISTENING

7 ▶17 Listen to Sam talking to George about George's holiday. Match the days to the weather.

1 Saturday   a snow
2 Sunday   b rain
3 Monday   c cloud
4 Tuesday   d thunderstorm
5 Wednesday   e sun
6 Thursday   f fog

Weather and places 65

Strange stories

VOCABULARY Talking about size

1 Put the letters in the right order to make words for talking about size.
1 g o l n ....
2 d w e i ....
3 p e d e ....
4 g i h h ....

2 Now complete the sentences with the words from Exercise 1.
1 We walked along Yonge Street in Toronto, but we couldn't walk along all of it because it's 1,896 kilometres ....
2 My brother and his friends climbed Mount McKinley in Alaska. It's 6,194 metres ....
3 We went to the Grand Canyon on our holiday to North America. It wasn't easy to see the bottom. It's 1,800 metres .... !
4 My friends and I wanted to swim across Lake Ontario, but it's 85 kilometres .... !

READING

3 Complete the five conversations. Choose A, B or C.

Example:
0 Shall we play tennis this afternoon?
A I can't because I've got a match.
B I didn't play tennis then.
C Yes, we watch it every day.

1 Whose bag is that?
A I don't know.
B It's not here.
C Isn't it?

2 Do you like swimming?
A I don't see it.
B That's not right.
C Yes, I do.

3 Were you at home yesterday?
A No problem.
B I live in a flat.
C Only in the morning.

4 Tom wasn't at school today.
A When was that?
B Do you know why?
C How old is he?

5 Where do you live?
A In Curitiba.
B Monterrey is nice.
C Five years.

WRITING

4 Complete the story with the past simple or past continuous form of the verbs.

Yesterday my family (1) .... (go) to the park for a picnic. 'We'll have a lovely time,' said Mum. 'May is the perfect month for football and a picnic in the park.'

But when we got to the park, it (2) .... (rain). 'Let's sit under this tree,' said Dad. We sat under the tree and (3) .... (eat) our cheese sandwiches and our cheese and onion crisps. But it was very cold. The wind was strong and the rain was heavy.

After an hour, it finally (4) .... (stop) raining. 'We'll have some sun now,' said Mum, 'and play football!' But then it started snowing!

'This is crazy,' said Mum, 'snow in May!'

'Right!' said Dad, 'let's go home and get warm.'

But as we (5) .... (walk) to our house, it stopped snowing. It was sunny and hot. There wasn't a cloud in the sky.

'I don't believe it!' said Mum. 'Right, everyone. Let's go to the house and get sunglasses, umbrellas and scarves. Then we can go back to the park. We'll be ready to play football in any weather.'

5 Read the story again and number the sentences in the right order.

  a They ate cheese sandwiches. ....
  b It started snowing. ....
  c It stopped raining. ....
  d They went to the park. ....
  e They went home. ....

6 Now write a story about the weather. Use the past simple and past continuous.

....
....
....
....
....
....

Weather and places

16 Amazing animals
He was looking at the gorillas ...

GRAMMAR Past simple / past continuous

1 Match the two halves of the sentences.

1 The girl was playing basketball
2 My parents were waiting for me
3 My cousin fell off his bike
4 When the teacher came back to the class,
5 While the boy was making a sandwich,
6 While I was looking at the website,

a he cut his finger.
b all the students were talking.
c when it started to rain.
d my laptop broke.
e while he was cycling round the park.
f at the airport when I got off the plane.

2 Write the sentences with *when* or *while*.

1 I was playing football I broke my leg. (when)
....

2 I was doing my maths homework, I fell asleep. (while)
....

3 My brother came home I was doing my homework. (while)
....

4 I was playing tennis, it started snowing. (while)
....

5 Dad was living in Sydney he met Mum. (when)
....

6 Sally was having lunch, her dad came home. (while)
....

3 Choose the right word to complete the sentences.

1 We *played / were playing* basketball when it started to rain.
2 I was walking through the park when I *found / was finding* the wallet.
3 Jo was making a pizza when she *cut / was cutting* her finger.
4 What *did you do / were you doing* yesterday afternoon at 3 pm?
5 I *saw / was seeing* Mr Smith the geography teacher while I was shopping with my mum.
6 While we *waited / were waiting* for the bus, my uncle drove past.

4 Number the events in the story in the right order.

a When I got to school, I lost my history book and my new pen. ....
b Yesterday wasn't a good day. Everything went wrong.
   While I was walking to school, it started to rain. I got very wet. ....
c After lunch we had a really hard maths test. ....
d While I was walking home, it started to rain again. I decided to run.
   But I dropped my English books onto the road. ....
e At lunchtime I was playing football when I fell and hurt my knee. ....
f I got home ten minutes later. I was very wet again and not happy. ....

68 Unit 16

5 Put the underlined verbs in the story into the past simple or past continuous.

It <u>is</u> Tuesday. It <u>is</u> very cold. I <u>am walking</u> down the street when I <u>see</u> a large gorilla in a baseball cap in front of me. 'Good morning,' <u>says</u> the gorilla.' 'Oh,' I <u>say</u>, 'good morning.' 'Don't worry,' <u>says</u> the gorilla. 'I'm not a real gorilla. I'm wearing a special gorilla suit.' The gorilla, who <u>is</u> really a man, <u>takes</u> his gorilla head off and <u>smiles</u>. 'It's very hot wearing this, you know,' he <u>says</u>.

It was Tuesday. ....
....
....
....
....
....
....
....
....
....
....
....
....
....

6 Students often make mistakes with the past continuous. Correct the mistakes in these sentences.

1 I was surprised when I was opening the presents yesterday morning.
....

2 I was watching a rugby competition on Saturday.
....

3 I was going to the shopping centre yesterday.
....

4 The weather was very nice but on December 23rd it was raining a lot.
....

5 I had a trip to Canada. I was going up the CN Tower.
....

Amazing animals 69

What can't these animals do!

VOCABULARY

1 Look at the pictures and write the words.

1 .... 2 .... 3 ....

4 .... 5 .... 6 ....

7 .... 8 .... 9 ....

READING

2 Read the article about bats. Choose the best word (A, B or C) for each space.

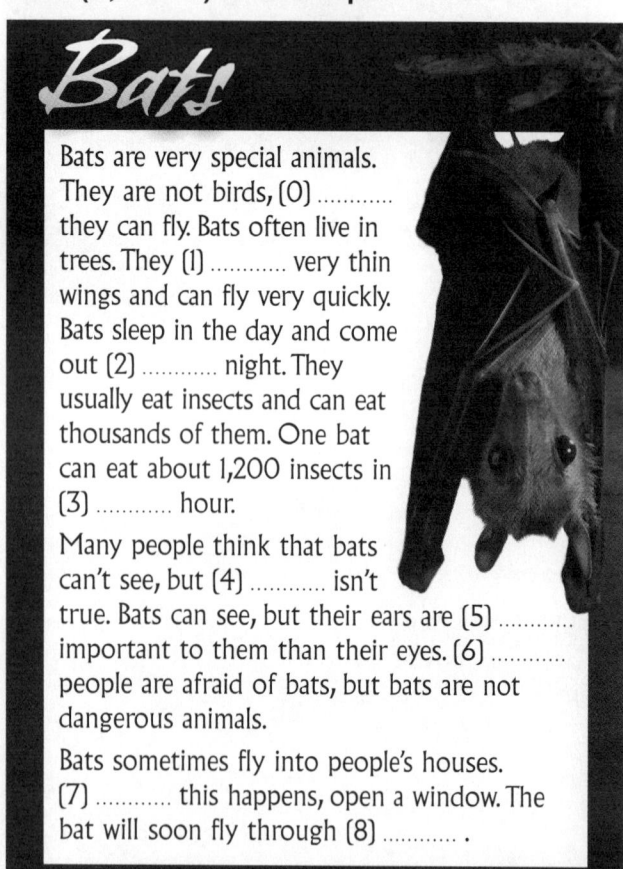

Bats

Bats are very special animals. They are not birds, (0) .... they can fly. Bats often live in trees. They (1) .... very thin wings and can fly very quickly. Bats sleep in the day and come out (2) .... night. They usually eat insects and can eat thousands of them. One bat can eat about 1,200 insects in (3) .... hour.

Many people think that bats can't see, but (4) .... isn't true. Bats can see, but their ears are (5) .... important to them than their eyes. (6) .... people are afraid of bats, but bats are not dangerous animals.

Bats sometimes fly into people's houses. (7) .... this happens, open a window. The bat will soon fly through (8) ....

Example:
0 Ⓐ	but	**B** so	**C** or
1 **A**	had	**B** has	**C** have
2 **A**	in	**B** at	**C** on
3 **A**	one	**B** both	**C** each
4 **A**	these	**B** that	**C** those
5 **A**	much	**B** most	**C** more
6 **A**	Some	**B** Any	**C** All
7 **A**	If	**B** And	**C** While
8 **A**	them	**B** it	**C** they

LISTENING

3 ▶18 Listen to Kirsty on the Animal World programme. Complete the text with the numbers in the box.

| 2 | 5 | 7 | 9 | 12 |

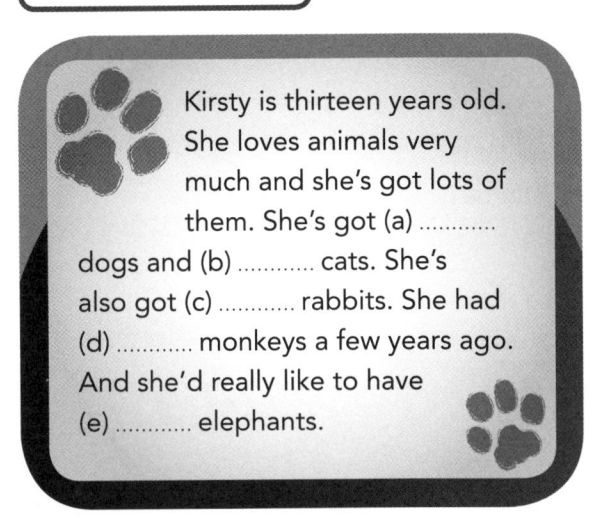

Kirsty is thirteen years old. She loves animals very much and she's got lots of them. She's got (a) .... dogs and (b) .... cats. She's also got (c) .... rabbits. She had (d) .... monkeys a few years ago. And she'd really like to have (e) .... elephants.

4 ▶18 Listen again. Tick (✔) the information you hear and cross (✘) the information you don't hear.

1 Kirsty lives with her grandparents. ....
2 Kirsty has got two brothers. ....
3 Kirsty has got two horses. ....
4 Kirsty loves her pet rat very much. ....
5 Kirsty wants to work with animals. ....

Prepare to write

5 Choose the right word or phrase to complete the sentences.

1 There are many types of wild animal, *for example / both* lions, tigers and elephants.
2 There are two types of elephant, the African and Indian. *Both / Also* of them are very big.
3 My grandmother has got lots of horses on her farm. She's *also / for example* got sheep.

6 Complete the description with *both*, *also* and *for example*.

My favourite animal

The rabbit is my favourite animal. There are many different types of rabbit, (1) .... the American Blue, the Florida White and the New Zealand Red. Rabbits eat a lot of grass. Grass is very important for rabbits. They (2) .... eat vegetables.

Our family has got two rabbits. (3) .... of the rabbits are very young. They don't live in the house with us because my parents don't like them to come into our kitchen or living room. The rabbits live at the bottom of the garden instead. I really enjoy playing with them after school.

7 Now write about your favourite animal.

....
....
....
....
....
....
....
....
....
....
....

Amazing animals

17 What's on? I'm going to record it

VOCABULARY

1 Match the two halves of the sentences.

1 What was
2 Did you
3 How many channels
4 The Disney Channel has
5 What's your
6 Which TV programmes are

a some great cartoons.
b does your TV have?
c record the film last night?
d favourite TV programme?
e you a fan of?
f on TV yesterday?

2 Complete the sentences with the words in the box.

cartoon   channel   fan   on   programmes   recorded

1 BBC 1 is a British TV ....
2 I didn't see the football match last night but I .... it.
3 *Family Guy* is a famous American ....
4 What's .... TV tonight? I hope there's something interesting.
5 What TV programmes do I like? I'm a big .... of sports programmes.
6 I didn't watch *The X-Factor*. I don't enjoy watching .... like that.

GRAMMAR   future with *going to*

3 Look at the pictures. What are the people going to do? Write sentences.

0 They're *going to play tennis*.
1 He .... 
2 She .... 
3 They .... 
4 He .... 
5 She .... 

Unit 17

4 Write complete sentences with *going to*.

1 He / not / visit his grandparents
   ....

2 I / visit my cousins
   ....

3 She / not / phone her friend
   ....

4 We / invite our friends
   ....

5 They / not / record the programme
   ....

6 We / not / go to the concert
   ....

5 Students often make mistakes with *going to*. Correct the mistakes in these sentences. Two of the sentences are correct.

1 She's going to meet us on Saturday afternoon.
   ....

2 I go to play tennis and football.
   ....

3 I'm happy because you going to come to my house.
   ....

4 They're going to travel around South Africa.
   ....

5 We going to get to the sports centre by car.
   ....

6 I hope you go have a lovely time in my town.
   ....

READING

6 Number the sentences in the right order.

a He watches it every evening for three or four hours. ....
b It's on the wall, opposite Eddie's bed. ....
c They would like him to read more in the evening. ....
d He prefers to read in the morning before school. ....
e My brother, Eddie, loves television. He has a TV in his room. .....1.....
f Talent shows are Eddie's favourite type of programme. ....
g He watches all of them. ....
h But my parents don't like Eddie watching talent shows. ....
i But Eddie doesn't like reading in the evening. ....
j The TV is very big. ....

7 Read the sentences in Exercise 6 again. Are these sentences right (✔) or wrong (✘)?

1 Eddie watches television in his room. ....
2 Eddie doesn't have a small television. ....
3 Eddie doesn't like reading. ....
4 Eddie watches some talent shows on television. ....
5 Eddie doesn't read in the evening. ....

What's your favourite TV show?

VOCABULARY Describing people

1 Find twelve words for describing people.

g	m	t	j	o	r	f	j
o	q	e	a	n	l	v	b
o	s	o	a	l	a	d	e
d	l	z	t	b	l	y	a
-	p	r	t	l	w	o	u
l	l	d	r	o	p	u	t
o	v	a	a	n	r	n	i
o	w	r	c	d	e	g	f
k	g	k	t	e	t	s	u
i	f	a	i	r	t	h	l
n	y	r	v	a	y	o	b
g	u	i	e	s	j	r	f
s	l	i	m	r	p	t	e

2 Complete the sentences with words from Exercise 1.

1. My cousin is very g…………………………. . He's going to be a model.
2. My brother is s…………………………. because he keeps fit and doesn't eat too much chocolate.
3. I'd like to play basketball, but I'm too s…………………………. .
4. When my father was a y…………………………. man, he wanted to be a doctor.
5. My grandmother is very o…………………………. .
6. You have to be t…………………………. to be a police officer.
7. We say that people with black hair are d…………………………. .
8. We usually use the word p…………………………. to describe women and girls, but not men and boys.

LISTENING

3 ▶19 You will hear five short conversations. There is one question for each conversation. For each question, choose the right answer (A, B or C).

Example:

0 What did Carlos do on Saturday evening?
A ☐   B ☐   C ✓

1 What does Jon's family like watching on TV?
A ☐   B ☐   C ☐

2 Which programme is Holly going to watch tonight?
A ☐   B ☐   C ☐

3 What time was the tennis match on television?
A ☐   B ☐   C ☐

4 How much was Tom's new TV?
A ☐ £50   B ☐ £100   C ☐ £250

5 Which programme did Rachel record?
A ☐   B ☐   C ☐

WRITING

4 Complete the blog with the words in the box.

> cartoon   Channel   fan   on TV   record

Tom's Cartoon Blog

I like watching cartoons very much. My favourite (1) .... is *The Simpsons*. It's very funny. *The Simpsons* is a famous American TV programme and I am a very big (2) .... of it. It's the story of a family in a small town in the United States. Homer and Marge are the parents of three children, Bart, Lisa and Maggie.

In the UK, you can watch *The Simpsons* on (3) .... Four. It's (4) .... every night. I watch it with my brother and sister. We (5) .... every programme because we like to watch them again and again.

5 Now read the blog again and answer the questions.

1. What country is *The Simpsons* from?
   ....
2. What type of TV programme is *The Simpsons*?
   ....
3. Who are Marge and Homer?
   ....
4. How many children are there in *The Simpsons*?
   ....
5. When is *The Simpsons* on TV?
   ....

6 Write about a cartoon that you like. Answer these questions:

1. What time is the programme on?
2. What channel is it on?
3. What is the programme about?
4. Why do you like it?

....
....
....
....
....
....

What's on?

18 Papers and magazines
Let's think of some ideas

VOCABULARY

1 Look at the pictures and write the words.

> advertisement   cartoon   magazine   newspaper   notice

1 ....
2 ....
3 ....
4 ....
5 ....

2 Complete the text with the words from Exercise 1. Use the plural form of two of the words.

> Hi Daniel,
>
> How are you? I'm working on the school (1) .... this year. I'm writing the book reviews. It's great fun. I wanted to draw the (2) .... too, but Sam's doing that. I love writing about books now. I'd like to write about books for a website or a (3) .... when I'm older. I sometimes look at job (4) .... online and think about the future. I'd like to work in London or New York!
>
> I saw a (5) .... at school today. It was for a party at the end of the year. Would you like to come?
>
> Right! I've got to go! See you soon!
>
> Judy

GRAMMAR   Making suggestions

3 Match the two halves of the sentences.

1 Why don't we   a we start a school magazine?
2 Let's   b watch the new cartoon on BBC 3 tonight?
3 Shall   c calling our online newspaper *The Buzz*?
4 How about   d stop. I'm tired.

4 Complete the conversation with the words in the box.

| about | don't | let's | not | shall |

George: Hi, Alba. Are you free this weekend?
Alba: Yes, I am. (1) .... we meet in the city and go shopping?
George: Good idea. I need some new shoes. How (2) .... going to the new department store next to the post office?
Alba: Excellent idea. It's got a great café. Why (3) .... we have lunch there?
George: Yes, OK. And (4) .... go to the cinema in the afternoon. I'd like to see the new James Bond film.
Alba: Hmm. I'd like to see the cartoon about the singing mouse.
George: OK. Why (5) .... see both?
Alba: Great!

5 Write five suggestions to make to a friend or family member for this weekend.

0 *Let's go skating this weekend.*
1 ....
2 ....
3 ....
4 ....
5 ....

6 👁 Students often make mistakes with the language for making suggestions. <u>Underline</u> three mistakes in the email.

> Hi Javi,
>
> How are you? Thanks for your email. Yes, I am free on Saturday. Lets go to the cinema! There is a new film I want to see. Why not to go to the cinema café before the film? They have great cakes! Why not we meet in front of the cinema at five o'clock? Is that OK for you?
>
> Love,
> Marina

7 Now correct the mistakes.

1 ....
2 ....
3 ....

LISTENING

8 ▶20 Jane calls a cinema and listens to a message. Match the numbers to the information. Which numbers does Jane choose?

1
2   **a** to hear about the café
     b to buy tickets
3   **c** to talk to an assistant
     d to hear about next week's new film
4   **e** to hear about this week's new film

Jane chooses numbers .... and ....

5

9 ▶20 Listen again and answer the questions.

1 What is the name of the cinema?
   ....
2 What is this week's film called?
   ....
3 How much are the tickets?
   ....
4 What is the name of the café?
   ....
5 What cakes can you buy in the café?
   ....

Papers and magazines 77

You should read it!

VOCABULARY as, because, so, when

1 Complete the sentences with *so*, *as*, *because* or *when*. You can use two words in two of the sentences.

   a I said, 'Wake up, Jake!' .... the play finished.
   b We wanted to watch the new play, ... we went to the theatre.
   c Jake didn't enjoy the play .... he was very tired.
   d I bought the tickets .... Jake didn't have any money with him.

2 Write the sentences from Exercise 1 in the right order.

   1 ....
   2 ....
   3 ....
   4 ....

WRITING

3 Complete the text about Roald Dahl. Write ONE word for each space.

   Example: 0 *of*

   I love all **(0)** .... Roald Dahl's books. My friends like **(1)** ....
   too. The books are very exciting and funny. He wrote **(2)** .... lot of famous
   books for children, teenagers **(3)** .... adults.

   Roald **(4)** .... born in South Wales in 1916, but **(5)** ....
   parents were **(6)** .... Norway. He wrote **(7)** .... a hut at
   the bottom of his garden. Today you can visit **(8)** .... Roald Dahl died in
   1990. He was 74 years **(9)** .... Children all over **(10)** ....
   world still read and love his stories.

4 Read the advertisement and the email to Alex. Fill in the information in Alex's notes.

WHAT'S ON at Frith Hall

(Shows at 7.30 p.m.)

Tuesday & Wednesday: Dancing Dolls
Thursday & Friday: Piano Evening

Tickets £19.50 (under 18s £12.30)
Phone 0153 667230 for information

Hi Alex

My Dad says he'll take us to Frith Hall. The concert sounds boring but there are good reviews for the other show! Dad can't do Tuesday. We'll leave our apartment at 6.45, but why not come earlier for pizza – is 5.30 OK? Text me on 08874 351299 if there's a problem.

Love Sam

ALEX'S NOTES

Name of theatre: Frith Hall

1 Show: ....
2 Day: ....
3 Time to be at Sam's home: ....
4 Price of my ticket: £ ....
5 Sam's phone number: ....

Prepare to write

5 Here are three reviews for a school magazine. Match the reviews to the titles.

1 I love this place. It's amazing! When you walk through the door, you see big photographs of famous people like Rafa Nadal and Jessica Ennis. There is something for everyone here: badminton, volleyball, hockey. The table tennis room is great! The sport centre is open from eight until nine seven days a week. I go there every day because I like to keep fit. See you there!

2 We went on Saturday. What's it like? Well, it's wonderful! We had ham and mushroom omelettes and cola. We got a table as we arrived really early. But this place is really popular, so it's a good idea to book a table. Oh, and don't forget. It's not open on Mondays.

3 I think the new TV show is boring. I know the show has lots of fans, but I'm not one of them. There's no story. I don't like watching actors singing old songs that I don't know. Anyway, it's on Channel 5 at 6 pm on Wednesdays.

a A Popular Café   **b** New on TV   **c** Sport for Everyone

6 Write a review for the magazine. Give your review a title.

19 School can be fun!
Do we have to wear our uniform?

VOCABULARY

1 Match the words to the examples.

1 activities   a   £300
2 cost   b   summer
3 uniform   c   four hours by train
4 journey   d   black trousers and white shirt
5 term   e   swimming, cycling, running

2 Put the words in the right order to make sentences.

1 term / end / of / a / there's / disco / the / at
....
2 activities / lots / can / we / different / do / of
....
3 towel / need / a / pack / we / to
....

GRAMMAR *have to / don't have to*

3 Look at the pictures and write sentences.

There are lots of rules at our school …

0 leave phones
We have to leave our phones at home.

1 be quiet
....

2 wear uniform
....

3 start school
....

4 go to school
....

5 learn Latin
....

4 Complete the sentences with the correct form of *have to*.

1 Andy .... do any homework today because he finished it all yesterday.
2 Sonya can't go to the cinema tomorrow because she .... look after her little brother.
3 We .... go to school tomorrow because it's Sunday.
4 My brother .... wear school uniform. He can wear jeans and a T-shirt to school.
5 I .... catch the bus to school because I can't walk there. It's too far.
6 My mum and dad .... go to work at the weekend. They can stay at home.

5 Students often make mistakes with *have to / don't have to*. Choose the right word to complete the sentences.

1 I *have / has* to do lots of homework for school.
2 You *has / have* to wear sports clothes.
3 *I've / I have* to buy a present for my sister.
4 It's warm here, but I think holidays *have / has* to be more interesting.
5 You *don't have to / haven't to* bring anything.
6 *We've to bring / We have to bring* a nature picture.

LISTENING

6 ▶21 **Listen to a conversation between Karl and Lucy about a school trip. Who says what? Write *K* for Karl or *L* for Lucy.**

0 Do you know what time we have to be at the airport?	....K....
1 Eight o'clock in the morning.	....
2 What about uniform?	....
3 I don't know.	....
4 I'm going to take chocolate, crisps and a cheese sandwich.	....
5 We have to take them for the football match.	....
6 It's going to be a great trip!	....

7 ▶21 **Listen again and answer the questions.**

1 Where are Karl and Lucy going on their school trip?
....
2 What time does the plane leave?
....
3 When are they going to play a football match?
....
4 What other sports can they play on their trip?
....

They don't have to study

VOCABULARY

1 Look at the pictures and write the words.

1 .... 2 .... 3 ....

4 .... 5 ....

2 Complete the sentences with the words from Exercise 1.

1 We can make our own sandwiches in the .... at our school.
2 You can learn how to make a website at my ....
3 They have a very big .... full of books at their school.
4 Can you play basketball in your school .... ?
5 We can't stay in the .... when we don't have lessons.

READING

3 Read the article about a school. Are the sentences 'Right' (A) or 'Wrong' (B)? If there is not enough information to answer 'Right' (A) or 'Wrong' (B), choose 'Doesn't say' (C).

Example:
0 Summer Tree Academy is a very small school.
   A Right   **B** Wrong   C Doesn't say

1 The school has more than one library.
   A Right   B Wrong   C Doesn't say

2 Summer Tree Academy is a new school.
   A Right   B Wrong   C Doesn't say

3 Students can only leave the school when they are eighteen.
   A Right   B Wrong   C Doesn't say

4 Students study photography if they want to.
   A Right   B Wrong   C Doesn't say

5 All students at Summer Tree Academy study Chinese.
   A Right   B Wrong   C Doesn't say

6 Teachers at the school can wear what they like.
   A Right   B Wrong   C Doesn't say

7 Boys and girls go to Summer Tree Academy.
   A Right   B Wrong   C Doesn't say

My brother's school is called Summer Tree Academy. It's a very big school in a small town in Western Australia. It has thirty-five classrooms, a few libraries and two gyms. It also has a large swimming pool. This school is very old. The first students went to Summer Tree Academy one hundred years ago. Some of the buildings are very beautiful.

People go to the school when they're twelve. They can leave when they're sixteen, or they can stay until they're eighteen. Students can study lots of different subjects. Everyone has to study English, maths and science, but they can also do drama, computer programming and photography. They don't have to study a language, but some students really enjoy learning Spanish and Chinese.

Students don't have to wear uniform at Summer Tree Academy. They can wear what they like, but they can only wear shorts if it's very hot. Teachers at the school believe that students enjoy school more if they don't wear uniform. My brother really enjoys going to the Summer Tree Academy and my little sister can't wait to start at the school.

WRITING

4 Complete the article with the words in the box.

| boys   children   schools   subjects   uniform |

Eton College is one of the most famous (1) .... in the world. It's in the south of England, near London. It isn't free to study at Eton. Parents pay around £30,000 a year to send their (2) .... to the school. The school is very big. More than 1,300 students study there. They're all (3) .... ! Students go to the school between the ages of thirteen and nineteen. Eton is a boarding school – the students sleep there.

Students at Eton have to wear a special (4) .... They wear long black coats, black trousers, white shirts, white ties and black hats.

Eton College students can learn many (5) .... Languages are very important. Every student has to study Latin for at least one year. Students at Eton can also do many sports, including rowing and tennis.

5 Read the article again and answer the questions.

1 Where is Eton?

....

2 How much does it cost to study at Eton?

....

3 How many students study there?

....

4 What type of school is Eton?

....

5 Which language do students have to study at Eton for at least one year?

....

6 Write about a famous school in your country. Find information about the school on the internet. Answer these questions.

1 What's the name of the school?
2 Where is it?
3 How big is it?
4 What subjects do you study?
5 What can students do there? What can't they do?
6 What do students have to do? What don't they have to do?

....
....
....
....
....
....

School can be fun!

20 Families
Her family worked hard

VOCABULARY

1 Complete the sentences with the words in the box.

> aunt   brother   cousin   grandfather
> grandmother   sister   uncle

1 Your mother's sister is your ....
2 Your mother's brother is your ....
3 Your father's mother is your ....
4 Your aunt's daughter is your ....
5 Your father's son is your ....
6 Your father's father is your ....
7 Your mother's daughter is your ....

2 Look at the family tree and answer the questions.

1 Who is George?
  Bill's ....
2 Who is Kathy?
  Bill's ....
3 Who is Margaret?
  Bill's ....
4 Who is Tara?
  Bill's ....
5 Who is Liam?
  Bill's ....
6 Who is Michael?
  Bill's ....

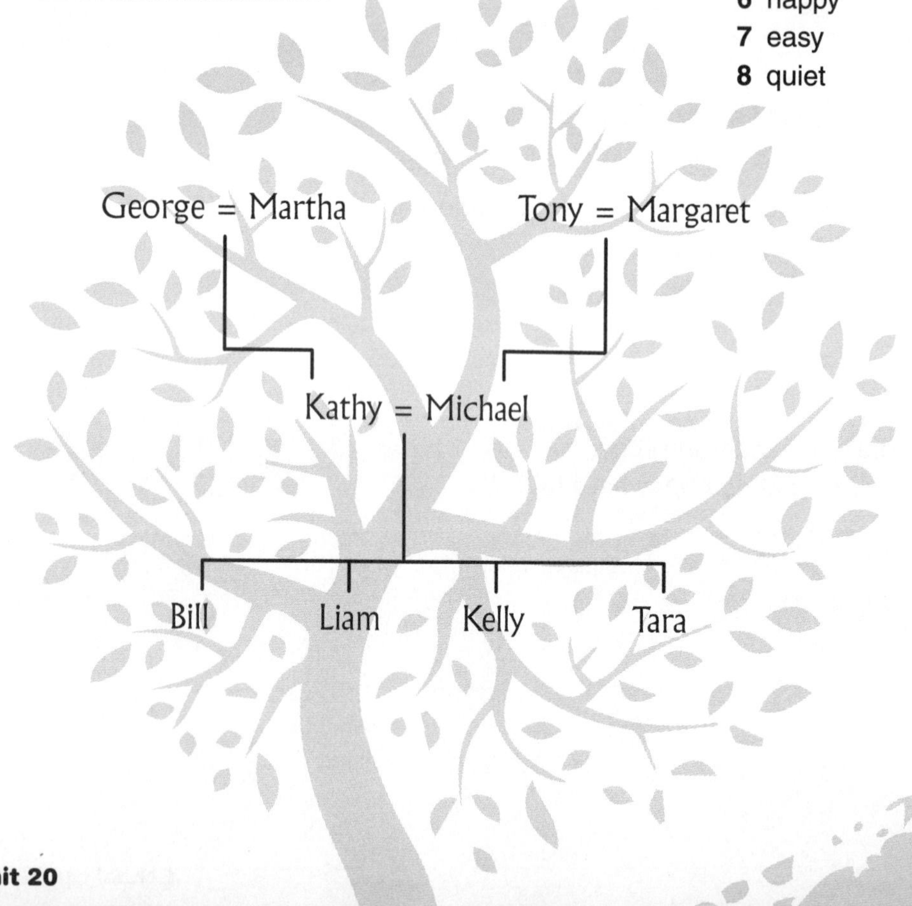

3 Write sentences about the family tree. Use the words in the box.

> daughter   granddaughter
> grandson   mother   son

1 Liam / Tony
  ....
2 Kelly / Michael
  ....
3 Tara / Martha
  ....
4 Bill / Kathy
  ....
5 Margaret / Michael
  ....

GRAMMAR   Adverbs of manner

4 Write the adverbs.

1 bad   ....
2 noisy   ....
3 wonderful   ....
4 careful   ....
5 quick   ....
6 happy   ....
7 easy   ....
8 quiet   ....

George = Martha   Tony = Margaret

Kathy = Michael

Bill   Liam   Kelly   Tara

5 Complete the sentences with the words in the box.

> badly   fast   hard   loudly   slowly   well

1 My brother isn't very happy. He did .... in his exams last week.
2 I don't swim very .... I never win any races in competitions.
3 Don't talk so .... , Josh. We have to be quiet in the library.
4 I worked really .... on my history project at the weekend.
5 I didn't do very .... in my chemistry test. My teacher wants me to do it again.
6 Come on! Why are you walking so .... ?

6 👁 Students often make mistakes with adverbs of manner. Correct the mistakes in these sentences.

1 We study together very happy.
....
2 Be carefully with the dog.
....
3 The team was playing very bad.
....
4 You can find my house very easy.
....
5 It was my favourite match because both teams played very hard.
....
6 I liked it a lot because the players played wonderful.
....
....

LISTENING

7 ▶22 Listen to Jonathan and match the family words to the names.

1 mother   a Anita
2 father   b Nicola
3 older sister   c Katie
4 younger sister d George
5 grandmother   e Mathew
6 uncle   f Sam

8 ▶22 Listen again and complete the text.

Jonathan's mother is
(1) .... years old. She's
a (2) .... and she works
very (3) .... Jonathan's
father is a writer. He writes books
for (4) .... Jonathan's
older sister is (5) ....
years old. His younger sister is
(6) .... years old.
Jonathan's grandmother is sixty-three.
She (7) .... Jonathan
lots of things. Jonathan's
(8) .... often comes to
stay at the weekend.

Families 85

Mother's Day is especially important

VOCABULARY Adverbs of degree

1 Choose the right word to complete the sentences.

1. **A:** What's your favourite hobby?
   B: I love reading books, *especially / nearly* books about sport.
2. **A:** How was the film?
   B: Well, it wasn't the best film, but it was *quite / really* good, I suppose.
3. **A:** Do you like the video game?
   B: Yes! It's *quite / really* good!
4. **A:** What do you think of our new music teacher?
   B: I *really / nearly* like him.
5. **A:** Phillip, hurry up! We have to go!
   B: OK. I'm *especially / almost* ready!
6. **A:** What time do we get there?
   B: Very soon, don't worry. We're *quite / nearly* there.

2 Complete the sentences with the words in the box.

> especially   nearly   quite   really

1. My sister .... likes playing tennis. She plays every day.
2. I like watching films, ... action films.
3. We go on holiday to France .... every year. We love it there.
4. I did .... well in my chemistry test. I got 65%.

READING

3 Read the sentences about John's older sister. Choose the best word (A, B or C) for each space.

Example:

0 John ...A... an older sister.
   A has   B takes   C gets

1 His sister .... to university last September.
   A stayed   B went   C arrived
2 Her .... subject at university is history.
   A favourite   B interesting   C popular
3 She really .... to be a teacher when she leaves university.
   A likes   B goes   C wants
4 John visited her for a weekend .... month.
   A that   B next   C last
5 They had a very .... time together.
   A good   B well   C better

Prepare to write

4 Choose the right word to complete the sentences.

1 I really like films. My sister likes them *too / also*.
2 I have a brother. I *also / as well* have a sister.
3 My grandmother lives with us. My grandfather lives with us *also / as well*.
4 I like playing basketball with my friends. I like playing tennis *too / also*.

5 Complete the text with *too* and *also*.

My brother is called Scott. He's fifteen years old. Scott is very tall and he has short black hair. Scott has lots of friends. He sees them in the evenings and at the weekends (1) ....
They go to the cinema and play football in the park.

Scott is a good student, but his favourite thing is music.

He loves listening to music. He (2) .... loves playing it. He plays the guitar. He plays the piano (3) .... He's a very good musician. Scott writes songs and plays other people's songs (4) .... He wants to be in a band when he leaves school.

He would also like to travel the world playing music.

6 Write about one member of your family (father, mother, sister, etc.). Use *too*, *also* and *as well*.

....
....
....
....
....
....
....

Families 87

Acknowledgements

Development of this publication has made use of the Cambridge English Corpus, a multi-billion word collection of spoken and written English. It includes the Cambridge Learner Corpus, a unique collection of candidate exam answers. Cambridge University Press has built up the Cambridge English Corpus to provide evidence about language use that helps to produce better language teaching materials.

This product is informed by English Profile, a Council of Europe-endorsed research programme that is providing detailed information about the language that learners of English know and use at each level of the Common European Framework of Reference (CEFR). For more information, please visit www.englishprofile.org

The authors and publishers acknowledge the following sources of copyright material and are grateful for the permissions granted. While every effort has been made, it has not always been possible to identify the sources of all the material used, or to trace all copyright holders. If any omissions are brought to our notice, we will be happy to include the appropriate acknowledgements on reprinting.

Photo acknowledgements

p. 5: Mike Flippo/Shutterstock; p. 6: Pressmaster/Shutterstock; p. 7: Gareth Boden; p. 10: (C) Image Source/Alamy; p. 11: (B/G) Duomo/Corbis, (TR) Studio DL/Corbis, (C) Christopher Futcher/Getty, (TC) Inti St Clair/Getty; p. 18: (B) David Grossman/Alamy; p. 20: (B) Iarigan – Patricia Hamilton/Getty; p. 23: (TL) Antiques & Collectables/Alamy, (TR) amana images inc./Alamy, (TC) photonic 17/Alamy, (BC) Image Source/Alamy, (LC) Image Source/Alamy; p. 24: (C) ZUMA Press, Inc./Alamy; p. 35: (TL) RIA Novosti/Alamy, (TC) James L. Stanfield/Getty, (BC) Iberfoto / SuperStock; p. 36: (1) D. Hurst/Alamy, (2) Image Source/Getty, (3) Paul Maguire/Alamy, (4) Pick and Mix Images/Alamy, (5) Bryan Mullennix/Getty, (6) Dim Dimich/Shutterstock, (7) K. Miri Photography/Shutterstock, (8) Richard Heyes/Alamy, (9) Shotshop GmbH/Alamy; p. 39: (B/G) Chad Riley/Getty; p. 46: (B) David Noton Photography/Alamy; p. 49: (B) elenaleonova/Getty; p. 51: (T) Kathrin Ziegler/Getty; p. 52: (C) Darrin Jenkins/Alamy; p. 55: (C) Iain Masterton/Alamy; p. 56: (B) Ivan Sedlak/Shutterstock; p. 58: (BL) Chris Willson/Alamy, (BR) Paul Cunningham/Corbis; p. 59: (B) Tony Tallec/Alamy; p. 64: (B) Doug McKinlay/Getty; p. 70: (B) Eureka/Alamy; p. 83: (TC) Photononstop/SuperStock; p. 86: (BL) Image Source/Corbis; p. 87: (C) Carey Kirkella/Getty.

Front cover photograph by R.legosyn/Shutterstock.

Illustrations

Ilias Arahovitis (Beehive Illustration) pp. 19, 22, 50, 72; Humberto Blanco (Sylvie Poggio Artists Agency) p. 4; Nigel Dobbyn (Beehive Illustration) pp. 21, 43, 65, 76, 78; Mark Draisey pp. 8, 26, 31, 37, 44, 53, 69, 73, 85; Mark Duffin pp. 28, 32, 36, 48; Richard Jones (Beehive Illustration) pp. 13, 16, 27, 47, 67, 70, 80, 82; Jamie Pogue (The Bright Agency) pp. 12, 14, 29, 34, 40, 42, 74; Martin Sanders (Beehive Illustration) p. 60

The publishers are grateful to the following contributors: text design and layouts: emc design Ltd; cover design: Andrew Ward; picture research: emc design Ltd; audio recordings: produced by IH Sound and recorded at DSound, London; edited by Liz Driscoll.